VICTORY IN THE
UNSEEN WARFARE

by Jack N. Sparks

D0879711

VICTORY IN THE
UNSEEN WARFARE

by Jack N. Sparks

adapted and arranged from the classic work
by Lorenzo Scupoli, *Spiritual Combat*,
as edited by Nicodemus of the Holy Mountain
and again by Saint Theophan the Recluse

CONCILIAR PRESS
Ben Lomond, California

VICTORY IN THE UNSEEN WARFARE
© 1993 Jack N. Sparks

Second Printing, 2000—Printed in Canada

Conciliar Press
P.O. Box 76, Ben Lomond, California 95005-0076

Library of Congress Cataloging-in-Publication Data

Sparks, Jack N.
    Victory in the unseen warfare / by Jack N. Sparks
        p.   cm.
    "Adapted and arranged from the classic work by Lorenzo Scupoli,
Spiritual combat, as edited by Nicodemus of the Holy Mountain and again
by Saint Theophan the Recluse."
    Includes index.
    ISBN 0-9622713-6-5 (pbk.)
    1. Spiritual life—Orthodox Eastern Church. 2. Spiritual warfare.
3. Perfection—Orthodox Eastern Church. 4. Orthodox Eastern Church—
Doctrines. 5. Orthodox Eastern Church—Membership. 6. Nicodemus,
the Hagiorite, Saint, 1748–1809. Aoratos polemos. 7. Feofan, Saint,
Bishop of Tambov and Shatsk, 1815–1894. I. Scupoli, Lorenzo, 1530–
1610. Combattimento spirituale. II. Title.
BX382.S64 1993
248.4'802—dc20   93-32708
                                             CIP

ACKNOWLEDGEMENTS

This volume is primarily based upon
selected chapters from:
Spiritual Combat
by Lorenzo Scupoli
as edited by Nicodemus of the Holy Mountain
and revised by Theophan the Recluse

I have worked for the most part from the translation by
E. Kadloubovsky and G.E.H. Palmer, first published in
England in 1952 by Faber and Faber under the title *Unseen
Warfare*, and later published in the United States by Saint
Vladimir's Seminary Press.

—Jack N. Sparks, Ben Lomond, California, 1993

TABLE OF CONTENTS

AN ESSENTIAL PREFACE

The book you are holding contains essential information for all Christians. Its use, however, requires a context: the Church and Orthodox spiritual guidance. No one should undertake to follow all that is said here without guidance. Everyone needs a spiritual father or guide.

A first reading of this volume can be puzzling. In one sense, it starts from the beginning, as if the reader were just beginning to inquire about following God. However, the content is so deep that any Christian, at any point in life, can receive help from starting at the beginning. And in another sense, this book is only for those who have become so serious about knowing God that everything else pales in comparison.

This is partly due to the fact that Scupoli's *Spiritual Combat* (first published in 1589) and the editions of *Unseen Warfare* which were developed from it came into being within a monastic context. The book is, therefore, a distillation of ascetic spiritual experience. Though the principles of spiritual warfare involved are the same for monastics and laity, there must undoubtedly be adaptations in application, for these are different kinds of lives. It is not our intent to replace *Spiritual Combat* or *Unseen Warfare* in their monastic application, but rather to produce a work which will be of assistance to lay Christians in developing their life with God.

7

BUILDING ON OUR BAPTISM

Yes, the work developed in a monastic context, where the only aim is to know God and become like Him. But there, at that exact point of entry, we also encounter its application to the life of every Christian.

Our baptismal vows amount to a total commitment to Christ, and it is to these vows, in fact, that the monastic pledge refers. In the Eastern Orthodox tradition, when we come for baptism, we are first asked: "Do you renounce Satan and all his works, and all his worship, and all his angels, and all his pride?" Three times this question is asked, and three times we answer, "I do."

Then, we are asked, "Have you renounced Satan?" Again, this question is asked three times, and three times we reply, "I have." We are asked to blow and spit upon Satan, and we do so. Next, we are asked, "Do you unite yourself to Christ?" This question is also asked three times, and three times we commit ourselves to Him: "I do." Immediately we are asked, "Have you united yourself to Christ?" And we emphatically reply, "I have." Finally, we are asked, "And do you believe in Him?" Our answer is, "I believe in Him as King and God." This we follow by repeating the Nicene Creed.

I mention these baptismal vows so we may see that at our baptism we committed ourselves absolutely to Christ, to unite ourselves to Him, to believe in Him as King and God. No greater commitment is possible. But what does it mean to make this commitment?

At the time of our baptism we probably know very little about how it can be practically worked out in our lives. (If baptized as infants, we have extremely little rational knowledge.) But we learn this step by step, if we follow Him. Once we begin to do so, our interaction with His commands, as given in the Sermon on the Mount, for example, is never-ending.

That is what this volume is all about—progress in our life with Christ. We cannot do it alone or outside the Church, for we need the Holy Mysteries, the wisdom of the Holy, Catholic, and Apostolic Church communicated to us through the guidance of our fathers, the companionship and encouragement of our brothers and sisters, and all the prayers of the faithful.

Consequently, the task set forth in this book must be seen as lifelong. That which cannot even be comprehended, let alone accomplished, at one stage in our spiritual journey will beckon us along sometime later. One thing we can do is to keep this volume, along with our Bible and prayer book, with us at all times, referring to it often, trusting that it will be continually useful—and that those parts which do not make sense or cannot be undertaken now will perhaps, somewhere in the future, have their day in our lives.

A BRIEF HISTORY OF THIS WORK

As was noted, this work derives from a classic of ascetic theology first published by the Italian monk, Lorenzo Scupoli, in 1589, as *Spiritual Combat*. The first edition, published in Venice, consisted of just twenty-four chapters, but successive editions were enlarged to first thirty-three, then thirty-seven, forty, and sixty-six chapters. During the seventeenth century editions were published under the name of John of Castanzia, a Spanish Benedictine monk. From the content, it is obvious that more than one man was involved in the book's development, and that it is a distillation of Christian ascetic spirituality.

During the latter half of the eighteenth century an Orthodox monk on Mount Athos, one Nicodemus (now called Nicodemus of the Holy Mountain), began translating *Spiritual Combat* into Greek, making adaptations and changes for the use of Orthodox Christians, adding, as he went, illustrations from the Scriptures and the writings of the Fathers. Among the monks on Mount Athos and among the people of the Orthodox Church in Greece, this adaptation, titled *Unseen Warfare*, became widely read and applied.

Later, in the nineteenth century, a copy of the Greek edition produced by Nicodemus came into the hands of Bishop Theophan the Recluse, a highly respected Russian theologian and spiritual director. Theophan translated *Unseen Warfare* into Russian, making additional changes he felt necessary for the benefit of the people with whom he worked. As a consequence, the work became widely distributed, read, and used in Russia, especially in the monasteries, but among the general populace as well.

The volume you see before you is offered as a modern adaptation of selected portions of this spiritual classic. Though in its preparation I have made use of the English translation of Scupoli's *Spiritual Combat* made in 1945 by William Lester and Robert Mohan, and published by Tan Books in 1990, I have paid closer attention to the translation of Theophan's Russian edition of *Unseen Warfare* by E. Kadloubovsky and G.E.H. Palmer, published by Faber and Faber of London in 1952 and later republished in the United States by Saint Vladimir's Seminary Press.

In addition, I have reorganized the material, combining chapters where appropriate, and arranging the content into three thematic divisions. (This volume represents only one third of the entire work. The other divisions cover prayer and virtue.) I have also added questions for thought or discussion at the end of each chapter. Though this work is designed primarily for personal study and use, I believe significant value can be gained from its use by small groups studying together. Therefore the questions are so constructed that they may be used either as personal study guides or as means of entering into group discussions.

CHAPTER 1

The Challenge of
Christian Perfection

As sincere Christians, we wish to be whatever God wants us to be—and ultimately, that means to be perfect. Our Lord commands: "Therefore you shall be perfect, just as your Father in heaven is perfect" (Matthew 5:48).

Saint Paul tells us, "Do not be children in understanding; however, in malice be babes, but in understanding be mature" (1 Corinthians 14:20). He also writes, "Epaphras . . . [labors] fervently for you in prayers, that you may stand perfect and complete in all the will of God" (Colossians 4:12). In another place we read, "Therefore, leaving the discussion of the elementary principles of Christ, let us go on to perfection, not laying again the foundation of repentance from dead works and of faith toward God" (Hebrews 6:1).

The command to strive for perfection is found in the Old Testament as well. In Deuteronomy God says to Israel, "You shall be blameless [or perfect] before the LORD your God" (Deuteronomy 18:13). David advises his son Solomon, "As for you, my son Solomon, know the God of your father, and serve Him with a loyal [or perfect] heart and with a willing mind; for the LORD searches all hearts and understands all the intent of the thoughts. If you seek Him, He will be found by you; but if you forsake Him, He will cast you off forever" (1 Chronicles 28:9).

We cannot fail to see from these examples that God calls for perfection on the part of Christians—that is, He wants us to be perfect in all virtues.

WHAT IS CHRISTIAN PERFECTION?

If we wish to reach such heights, we must first learn what constitutes Christian perfection. If we have not learned this lesson, we may turn away from the right path and go off in a different direction, thinking all the while that we are progressing toward perfection.

Here is the truth we must absorb: The greatest and most perfect thing a human being can ever desire to achieve is to come near to God and dwell in union with Him.

Some people—those who judge by appearances—say the perfect Christian life consists in carrying out fasts, vigils, and prostrations, sleeping on bare earth, and similar severities of the body. Others will say it consists in saying many prayers at home and attending long services in church. Still others think perfection consists entirely of mental prayer, solitude, isolation, and silence.

The majority, however, will say perfection comes only by strictly observing all the rules and practices of the tradition, neither going overboard nor being deficient, but keeping to a sort of "golden moderation."

So we see that, by and large, people judge perfection by the external standard of observance of certain practices. But all the virtues mentioned above do not, in and of themselves, constitute the Christian perfection we are seeking. They are only means and methods designed to help us acquire it—and they may or may not do so.

There is, of course, no doubt these things do help some people to attain perfection in the Christian life. There are virtuous people who practice these virtues as they should, to acquire strength and power against their own sinful tendencies. Through these practices, they gain courage to withstand the temptations and seductions of our three main enemies:[1] the world, the flesh, and the devil. By using these means properly, and at the right time, they gain the spiritual support so necessary to all servants of God, and especially to beginners.

These virtuous people practice piety, each as is appropriate for himself. They may fast to subdue their unruly flesh, practice vigils to sharpen their inner vision, and sleep on uncomfortable surfaces to keep their minds and bodies from becoming soft through too much sleep. They may practice silence and go into solitude to avoid any enticement to offend the All-Holy God. They also recite prayers, attend church services, and carry out other acts of devotion in order to keep their minds on heavenly things.

In addition, they read of the life, suffering, and death of our Lord for the sole purpose of understanding more clearly their own deficiencies and the merciful loving-kindness of God. This reading helps them desire and learn to follow the Lord Jesus Christ, bearing their cross with self-denial. It also strengthens their love of God as they learn to abhor their own sinfulness.

PITFALLS OF DECEPTION
On the other hand, these same activities may do more harm than good to those who take them as the sole basis

of their life and their hope. It is also dangerous to undertake them independently or inappropriately, without the direction of a spiritual father or guide. The harm can come, not from the nature of the deeds, but through the fault of those who use them improperly—giving attention only to the external practice, allowing their hearts to be moved only by their own will and the will of the devil. In their case the devil, seeing that they have left the right path, gleefully refrains from interfering with their activities, even allowing them to increase and multiply their efforts in obedience to their vain ideas.

Experiencing certain spiritual stirrings and comforts along with their pious activities, such people begin to imagine they have already attained the condition of the angels and to feel that God Himself is present in them. At times, in fact, engrossed in the contemplation of abstract and unearthly things, they imagine they have completely transcended this world and have been transported to the third heaven.

Nevertheless, Christians who examine the life and character of such people can clearly see how sinfully they behave and how far they are from true perfection. As a rule, people who rely on their righteous deeds as their sole basis of life and hope display certain discernible characteristics:

• They always wish to be considered better and more important than other people.

• They want their own way and are stubborn in their decisions.

• They are blind in everything concerning themselves,

but are very clearsighted when it comes to examining the words and actions of others.

If someone else is held by others in the same esteem these people think they enjoy (or should enjoy), they cannot bear it and become openly hostile to that person. And if anyone interferes with them in their pious activities, God forbid! They immediately become indignant, boil over with anger, and become quite unlike what they are believed to be.

If, desiring to bring them to a knowledge of themselves and to lead them on the right path to perfection, God sends them afflictions and sickness—or allows them to be persecuted, the means by which He ordinarily tests His true and real servants—this test immediately shows what is hidden in their hearts and how deeply they are corrupted by pride. For whatever affliction comes upon them, they refuse to bend their necks to the yoke of God's will and to trust in His secret and righteous judgments. They do not want to follow the example of our Lord Jesus Christ, Son of God, who humbled Himself and suffered for our sakes. They refuse to be humble, to consider themselves the lowest of all creatures, to regard their persecutors as good friends, tools of God's generosity toward them and helpers in their salvation.

Thus, it is clear such people are in great danger. Their inner eye, that is, their spirit,[2] is darkened, and looking at themselves through it, they see incorrectly. Remembering their external pious works and considering them good, they imagine they have already reached perfection. Puffing themselves up, they begin to judge others. After this it is impossible for anyone to convert such people, except through God's special influence. An obvious sinner will turn toward good much more easily than will a secret sinner who hides under the cloak of visible virtues.

DRAWING NEAR TO GOD

Now, having seen clearly and definitely that spiritual life and perfection do not consist in these visible virtues of which we have written, we must learn in what they do consist: in coming near to God and dwelling in union with Him, as we said at the very beginning.

Along with this will come a heartfelt realization of the goodness and greatness of God, together with consciousness of our own weakness, inability, and susceptibility to sin. We must love God and feel remorse for our sins, humbling ourselves not only before God but also before all people, for the sake of our love of God. We must renounce all will of our own and learn perfect obedience to the will of God. Finally, we must desire all these things with a pure heart, to the glory of God (1 Corinthians 10:31), from sheer desire to please God—because He Himself wishes it and because we should so love Him and work for Him.

This is the law of love, which the Holy Spirit Himself has written on the hearts of the faithful. This is the self-denial our Savior calls for so earnestly in the Gospels. This is the blessed yoke of Jesus Christ and His burden that is light. This is the submission to God's will which our Redeemer and Teacher demands from us both by His word and by His example.

Did not our Master, the Author of our salvation, our Lord Jesus Christ, tell us to say when praying to the heavenly Father, "Our Father . . . Your will be done on earth as it is in heaven" (Matthew 6:9, 10)? And did not He Himself exclaim on the eve of His suffering and death, "Not My will, but Yours, be done" (Luke 22:42)? And did He not say of His whole work, "For I have come down from heaven, not to do My own will, but the will of Him who sent Me" (John 6:38)?

Do you now see what all this means, brothers and sisters? Like most sincere Christians, you are probably already expressing your readiness and are longing to reach the height of such perfection. Blessed be your zeal! But prepare yourself for labor, sweat, and struggle, beginning with your very first steps on the path. You must sacrifice everything to God and do only His will. You will meet within yourself a multitude of desires, all clamoring for satisfaction, whether or not it agrees with the will of God. Nor can you reach perfection all at once—sometimes a lifetime is required.

Therefore, to reach our chosen aim, we must first curb our own desires, submitting them to the will of God. In order to succeed in this, we must constantly oppose all evil in ourselves and urge ourselves toward good. In other words, we must ceaselessly fight against ourselves and against everything that arouses and supports our sinful passions.[3] So prepare yourself for this struggle and this warfare, knowing the crown—the attainment of your desired aim—is given to none but the most courageous of those who go to war.

WEAPONS FOR VICTORY

But if this is the hardest of all wars—since it is within ourselves that we meet opposition—victory in it is the most glorious of all. And, what is most important, it is the most pleasing to God. If, inspired by devotion, we overcome and put to death our unruly passions—our sinful lusts and desires—we will please God more and will work for Him more beautifully than if we whip ourselves till we draw blood, or exhaust ourselves by fasts more than any ancient hermit of the desert.

On the other hand, not even the most magnificent good deed will save us if we remain slaves to our passions. Indeed, whatever work we may undertake, however glorious, will not lead us to our desired aim if we give our passions free rein, allowing them to live and act within us.

Finally, if after learning what constitutes Christian perfection, and realizing that to achieve it you must wage a constant, cruel war with yourself, you really desire to be victorious in this unseen warfare and be rewarded with a crown, you must plant in your heart the following four dispositions and spiritual activities. You must arm yourself with these invisible weapons, the most trustworthy and unconquerable of all:

• Do not rely on yourself in the spiritual warfare.

• Bear always in your heart a perfect and all-daring trust in God alone.

• Strive without ceasing.

• Remain constantly in prayer.

STUDY QUESTIONS

WHAT IS CHRISTIAN PERFECTION?

1. Be sure you understand the definition of Christian perfection. Try to give it in one brief sentence.
2. Consider the things many people think constitute the perfect Christian life. Why would they think this way? Consider what Scripture says concerning each of these practices.
3. What is the value of those virtuous practices considered so important? Consider them one by one. What role can they play in making us what God wants us to be?

PITFALLS OF DECEPTION

1. What is the danger in misuse of these virtuous practices?
2. What are some signs of their misuse? What danger signs should we look for in ourselves?
3. How can we help ourselves when we see we are in such danger?

DRAWING NEAR TO GOD

1. Consider those qualities of heart, soul, and spirit which are connected with perfection. What is their distinguishing mark?

WEAPONS FOR VICTORY

1. How can we make ourselves ready for the pursuit of Christian perfection, for the unseen warfare?

CHAPTER 2

Trusting God in the Spiritual Warfare

AVOID SELF-RELIANCE IN SPIRITUAL WARFARE

The nature of our struggle requires that we learn not to rely on ourselves.[4] This requirement, beloved brothers and sisters, is absolutely essential to the victory. You must be certain of this: if you rely on yourself you will be unable to resist the smallest attack of the enemy. Engrave this truth deeply in your spirit and heart.

Despite the weakening of our spiritual and moral powers that resulted from the transgression of our forefather Adam, we are inclined to think very highly of ourselves. Even though our daily experience proves to us very effectively that this opinion of ourselves is false, we continue to believe that we are something and, indeed, something very important.

Nevertheless, this spiritual disease of ours, which is so difficult for us to grasp and admit, displeases God more than anything and everything else about us. It is the first product of our selfishness and self-love—and the source of all sinful passions, as well as of all our spiritual failures and sinful deeds. It closes the very door of our spirit, the only opening through which divine grace can enter, giving this grace no way to come and dwell in us. So we are left without the very grace we need so much.

For how can grace, which comes to help and enlighten us, enter someone who thinks that he is something great—that he knows everything and needs no outside help? May God preserve us from this disease and passion of Lucifer!

God severely reprimands those who are under the sway of this passion of pride and self-admiration, saying through the prophet: "Woe to those who are wise in their own eyes, and prudent in their own sight" (Isaiah 5:21). And the Apostle Paul tells us: "Be of the same mind toward one another. Do not set your mind on high things, but associate with the humble. Do not be wise in your own opinion" (Romans 12:16).

While God abhors this sinful charade and foolishness on our part, there is nothing He loves and desires to see in us more than a sincere consciousness of our insignificance and inability, together with a firm and deeply felt conviction that any good we may have in our life comes from Him alone, since He is the source of all good.

Therefore, He carefully plants this heavenly seed in the hearts of His beloved friends, urging them not to hold themselves in esteem nor to rely upon themselves. Sometimes He does this by means of grace and inner illumination; sometimes through difficulties and tribulation from the outside world; sometimes through unexpected and almost irresistible temptations; and sometimes by other means, not always discernible by us.

Although the virtue of expecting no good from ourselves and not relying on ourselves is something God works in us, we must still, on our part, make every effort

23

within our power to acquire this frame of mind. Here are four activities by means of which, with God's help, we may finally acquire disbelief in ourselves, learning never to rely on ourselves in anything:

• We must realize our own lack of ability, constantly keeping in mind that by ourselves we can do nothing good worthy of the Kingdom of heaven. Listen to the words of the wise Fathers: Peter of Damascus assures us, "Nothing is better than to realize one's weakness and ignorance. And nothing is worse than not to be aware of them" (*Philokalia*). Saint Maximus the Confessor teaches: "The foundation of every virtue is the realization of human weakness" (*Philokalia*). Saint John Chrysostom says: "He alone knows himself in the best way possible who thinks of himself as being insignificant."

• We must ask for God's help in this with fervent and humble prayers, for this is His gift. And if we wish to receive it, we must first instill in ourselves the conviction that not only do we lack such consciousness of ourselves, but we cannot acquire it by our own efforts. Then, standing boldly before Almighty God, in the firm belief that in His great lovingkindness He will grant us this knowledge of ourselves—when and how He alone knows—we must not let the slightest doubt creep in that we will actually receive it.

• We must accustom ourselves to be wary, fearing our innumerable enemies (the devil and his demons), whom we cannot resist for even a short time. Fear their long experience in battling us, their cunning, their ambushes, their power to assume the appearance of angels of light, and their numerous tricks and traps, which they secretly spread on the path of our life of virtues.

• If we fall into some transgression, we must quickly turn to the realization of our weakness and be aware of it. For God allows us to fall for the very purpose of making us more aware of our weakness—so we may learn not only to distrust ourselves, but also, because of our weakness, to wish to be distrusted by others as well. Learn this: without such desires it is impossible for this beneficial disbelief in our own abilities to be born and take root within us. And this disbelief is the foundation and beginning of true humility, since it is based on the realization, by experience, of our impotence and unreliability.

From the above we may see how necessary it is for someone who desires to participate in heavenly light to know himself. We also see how God's mercy usually leads the proud and self-reliant to this knowledge through their downfall—justly allowing them to fall into the very sin from which they think they are strong enough to protect themselves. In that way He enables them to see their weakness and prevents them from foolishly relying on themselves.

Though this method is very effective, it is also dangerous, and God does not always use it. He does so only when all the other means we have mentioned (which are easier and more natural) fail to lead us to self-knowledge. Only then will He allow us to fall into sin, great or small, depending on the degree of our pride, vanity, and self-reliance. Consequently, where conceit and self-reliance are absent, such instructive failures do not occur.

Therefore, if you happen to fall, run quickly in your thoughts to humble self-knowledge and a low opinion of and attitude toward yourself, imploring God by persistent prayer to give you true light—enabling you to recognize your emptiness and insignificance, confirming in your heart a settled disbelief in yourself—lest you fall again into the same, or an even worse and more destructive sin.

We must add that not only when you fall into some sin, but also when you are afflicted by hardship, tribulation, or sorrow—especially by a painful and long-lasting bodily illness—you must understand that you suffer this in order to acquire self-knowledge (namely the knowledge of your weakness) and to become humble. It is also with this purpose that God allows us to be assaulted by all kinds of temptation, from the devil, from other people, and from our own tendencies to sin. Saint Paul saw this purpose in the trials and temptations he suffered in Asia Minor, when he wrote: "We had the sentence of death in ourselves, that we should not trust in ourselves but in God who raises the dead" (2 Corinthians 1:9).

There is one thing more to be added: If you want to prove your weakness from the actual experience of your life, then observe closely—for just one day—your own thoughts, words, and actions. You will find that most of them are sinful, wrong, foolish, and bad. This experiment will make you understand in practice how far you are from God and how weak you are in yourself. This understanding will make you feel how foolish it is, if you truly wish yourself well, to expect anything good from yourself or to rely on yourself.

BE CONFIDENT IN GOD ALONE

We have said it is very important not to rely on our own efforts in this unseen warfare. Still, if we merely give up all hope of ourselves, despairing of our own ability to succeed in the spiritual warfare without having found another source of support, we have no choice but to flee the battle-field immediately—or be overcome and taken prisoner by our enemies.

Therefore, along with complete renunciation of our own abilities, it is necessary to plant in our hearts a perfect trust in God and absolute confidence in Him. That is, we must know and feel with our whole heart that we have no one but God to rely on—and that we can expect every kind of good, every means of help, and victory as well, from Him alone.

Since in ourselves we totally lack the capacity to pursue this warfare, we can expect from ourselves nothing but stumbling and falling—which leave us no hope of victory. If, on the other hand, we arm our heart with a living trust in God and an unshakable certainty that we will receive His help, we are certain always to be granted victory by Him. We are assured of this by the psalm: "The LORD is my strength and my shield; my heart trusted in Him, and I am helped; therefore my heart greatly rejoices, and with my song I will praise Him" (Psalm 28:7).

The following thoughts can help us to become grounded in this hope—and thereby prepare us to receive help.

We seek this help from God, who is omnipotent and can do all He chooses. It follows, therefore, that He can certainly help us. Being omniscient and wise, He knows everything perfectly. He knows, therefore, fully and completely, all that is best for the salvation of each of us. God is also infinitely good and comes to us with love so profound and perfect as to be indescribable. He always desires, and is ready from hour to hour and moment to moment, to give us all the help we need for complete victory in the spiritual warfare taking place within us—as soon as we run with firm trust to the protection of His arms.

And consider this also. Our Good Shepherd, who for three years walked the earth, searched for sheep who had gone astray, called for them so loudly that His throat became parched, following paths so hard and thorny that He shed all His blood and gave up His life. How is it possible that now—if His sheep follow Him, turn to Him with love, and call for His help with hope—He should fail them? No! He turns His eyes to His lost sheep, takes them into His divine arms, and, placing them among the heavenly angels, makes a welcoming feast for their sake!

If our God never ceases to search diligently and lovingly for the blind and deaf sinner (like the woman who searched for the piece of silver in the Gospel, Luke 15:8-10), how could we possibly believe He would abandon that poor sinner now, when, like a lost sheep, he cries out for his Shepherd?

Who, indeed, will ever believe that God, who according to John's Revelation, constantly stands at the door of our heart and knocks, wishing to come in and dine with us (Revelation 3:20), and bestow gifts upon us—who will believe that this same God would be deaf and refuse to enter if we open the door of our heart to Him and invite Him in?

We must therefore add to the above yet another method of bringing to life within us a firm trust in God— and of gaining His speedy help. That method is to review in our memory all the instances of speedy divine help described in the Scriptures. These instances, which are so numerous, show us clearly that no one who put his trust in God was ever left ruined, perplexed, defeated, and without help. "Consider the generations of old," says the wise Sirach, "has anyone trusted in the Lord and been disappointed?" (Ecclesiasticus 2:10).

Armed, then, with all of these weapons, we may enter the battle with courage and wage war watchfully, with full conviction that victory will be granted. For with their help we will most certainly acquire perfect trust in God—and this trust will never fail to attract God's help, and provide us with unconquerable power. These two together will, in the end, cause complete distrust of ourselves to become deeply rooted within us.

We are taking every possible opportunity to remind you to distrust yourself. We know no one who does not need that reminder constantly, since self-esteem is so deeply rooted in us. It is so firmly enmeshed in us—making us think we are something, even something important— that it always hides in our heart, a subtle and imperceptible presence, even when we are sure we do not trust ourselves and are, on the contrary, filled with complete trust in God alone.

In order to avoid this foolish pride of heart and act without any self-reliance, led only by your trust in God, always take care to maintain an attitude in which the consciousness and feeling of your weakness are in the forefront of your awareness as you contemplate the all-powerfulness of God. And keep both alike before you in everything you do.

DISTINGUISHING SELF-RELIANCE FROM TRUST IN GOD

People who are relying on themselves in spiritual warfare often think they have no self-reliance—that they have put all their trust in God, resting confidently in Him alone. But the truth is far different. We can see the truth ourselves if we judge by what we are like inside and by what happens there if we fall down.

If, when we grieve at our downfall, reproaching and scolding ourselves for it, we think: "I shall do this and that, then the consequences of my downfall will be wiped out and everything will be all right once again," this is a sure sign that before our downfall we trusted ourselves, instead of trusting God—and that we are continuing to do so!

Here is the test: the more gloomy and depressed we are in our grief, the more it can be seen that we relied too much on ourselves and too little on God. When that is the case, the grief caused by our downfall is not moderated by any comfort. On the other hand, if we do not rely on ourselves but put our trust in God, when we fall we are not greatly surprised, nor are we overcome with excessive grief, for we know this fall is the result of our own impotence—and above all of the weakness of our trust in God. Thus, our downfall increases our distrust of ourselves and makes us try even harder to increase and deepen our humble trust in God.

Further, hating the corrupt passions which caused our downfall, we undergo peacefully and calmly the work of repentance necessary for having offended God. Armed with still more trust in God, we pursue our enemies with the greatest of courage and resolve—even unto death.

Let us reflect carefully on these truths—especially if we think ourselves virtuous and spiritual (we know if we do!), and especially if, when we fall into some sin, we are overcome with anxiety and torment, finding no peace anywhere. Exhausted by this grief and anxiety—which we suffer for no other reason but self-esteem—we run, again urged by self-esteem, to our spiritual father, to be freed of this burden. The fact is, we should have gone to him immediately after the downfall, for no other reason but a desire to wash away as quickly as possible the filth of sin which has offended God—and to acquire new strength to fight against our sinful passions by means of the most holy sacrament of repentance and confession.

STUDY QUESTIONS

AVOID SELF-RELIANCE IN SPIRITUAL WARFARE

1. *What is your first reaction to the advice not to rely on yourself, to esteem yourself insignificant? Does it seem odd that God would want us to consider ourselves inept and unable to make progress toward becoming good?*
2. *What is the disease discussed? How can it handicap our*

relationship with God? How can it hinder what God wants to do with us?

3. *Consider the four activities given as aids toward acquiring disbelief in yourself. How do these fit together to help you along on this first step of spiritual discovery? How might you apply them in your own life?*

4. *Try the experiment described on page 26. What do you discover about yourself? In what ways are you out of harmony with God (and yourself)?*

BE CONFIDENT IN GOD ALONE

1. *Discuss the ways in which distrust in our own abilities and trust in God are corollary to each other.*

2. *Consider the parables of Jesus relating to His seeking for the lost—especially the three in Luke 15:1-32. How do these help you to feel secure in His love? Are there ways in which they also inspire you to turn to Him for hope and help?*

3. *Choose at least one instance of "speedy divine help described in the Scriptures." Consider how this example can help you develop confidence in God.*

DISTINGUISHING SELF-RELIANCE
FROM TRUST IN GOD

1. *What is one sure sign that we are relying on ourselves rather than on God? How does trust in God change this?*

2. *How does our response to a fall affect our future trust in God?*

3. *What is the value of immediately seeking the sacrament of repentance and confession when we fall?*

CHAPTER 3

A Good Soldier of Jesus Christ

THE PROPER SCOPE OF SELF-DISTRUST

Since all our strength for overcoming our enemies is acquired through disbelief in ourselves and trust in God, it is necessary for us to understand these things thoroughly. This will help us always to have that strength and to preserve it with the help of God.

We must understand, and never forget, that neither all our capabilities and good qualities, whether natural or acquired; nor all the gifts freely given us; nor the knowledge of all the Scriptures; nor the fact that we have long worked for God and have acquired experience in all these labors; nor even all these things together will enable us to rightly do God's will. That is to say, these capabilities will not help us unless for every good deed pleasing to God that we are about to undertake, for every affliction we wish to avoid, for every cross we have to bear according to God's will—unless, on all these occasions and similar ones, a special divine help inspires our heart to give us strength to accomplish it. As the Lord said: "Without Me you can do nothing" (John 15:5).

Therefore, for the rest of our life, every day and every moment, we must keep unchanged in our heart the feeling, conviction, and frame of mind that never on any occasion can we allow ourselves to think of relying on and trusting in ourselves in this spiritual warfare.

With respect to trust in God, we may add the following to that given before: we must know and understand that nothing is easier for God than to give us victory over our enemies—whether they be few or many, whether they be old and strong, or new and weak.

Yet He has His own time and order for everything. Therefore, we must never weaken in our trust of God or fall away from Him. Though a soul be overburdened with sins, though it be guilty of all the crimes in the world, though it be defiled beyond all imagination, that soul must trust in God. If that same soul uses every means and endeavor to become free of sin and turn to the path of good, but cannot get stabilized in anything upright, and even sinks ever deeper into evil, still that soul must continue to trust.

That soul must not abandon its spiritual weapons and labors, but must fight and fight, struggling with itself—and with its enemies—with all its courage and with untiring effort. We must know and understand that in this unseen war, all are losers except that person who never ceases to struggle and to keep faith in God. For God never abandons those who fight in His armies—although at times He allows them to suffer wounds.

So let us fight, all of us, and not give ground; for the whole issue is wrapped up in this unceasing struggle. God is always ready with assistance and care for those struck down by the enemies—and with help for overcoming those enemies, help which He sends His warriors in due time if they seek Him and firmly hope in Him. At some hour when they least expect it, they will see their proud enemies vanish, as it is written: "The mighty men of Babylon have ceased fighting . . . the bars of her gate are broken" (Jeremiah 51:30).

AVOID WORRYING AND A RESTLESS HEART

Just as when we lose our peace of heart, it is our duty to do all we can to restore it, we are no less obligated to prevent the accidental happenings of life from disturbing this peace. By this I mean such happenings as illness, wounds, deaths of relatives, wars, fires, sudden joys, fears and sorrows, memories of former sins and errors—in a word, all those things which ordinarily trouble and agitate our heart.

In such cases we simply must not allow ourselves to become worried and agitated. Once we give in to agitation, we lose both self-control and the ability to understand events clearly in order to do the right thing. Each such loss gives the devil another avenue to agitate us still more and push us to take some step which would be difficult or even impossible to remedy.

It is not that we should refuse to let sorrow come—we cannot stop it. But do not let sorrow take possession of your heart and agitate it. Keep it outside the bounds of your heart and quickly soften and restrain it so it cannot prevent you from reasoning soundly and acting correctly. With God's help, this much is within our power—if we maintain a determined spiritual frame of mind and a firm intent to keep a proper attitude.

Each hardship we may suffer has its own character-istics and each requires its own remedies. Nevertheless, there are some things we can say in general, because all hardships have one thing in common: they all trouble and agitate our soul. There is one thing we can always do to help us in any kind of trouble. That is, have faith in the good Providence of God, who arranges the course of our life, with all its accidental happenings, for our good.

Along with that faith, we must also maintain a serene submission to God's will, expressing that submission in an attitude which causes us to call from the bottom of our heart: "Let God's will be done! For His will is our good."

Different people experience and recognize this good differently. One person recognizes: This goodness of God leads me to repentance. Another feels: It is because of my sins that the Lord has sent me this trial—to purify me of them. I am experiencing God's purging. A third thinks: The Lord is testing me to see whether I'm serving Him sincerely. And those who look from the outside at a person experiencing adversity may think a fourth way: This trial is sent to this person so that the works of God may be revealed in him.

But such a verdict as that last one can only be rendered when hardship and affliction are over—when God's help is evident in the soul of the afflicted person. Only the first three feelings have validity in the midst of trials. No matter which of them enters our heart, each has the virtue and strength to quiet the rising storm of sorrow and establish peace and good cheer in our heart.

Here is a general means for making peace in your heart when some affliction tries to disturb it:

• With all your strength make firm your faith in the

goodness of God's Providence for you.

• Next, revive in your soul a loyal submission to God's will.

• Then, introduce into your heart the reflections set forth above and urge it to feel that the hardship you suffer at this moment is either a means by which the Lord is testing you, or His means of urging you to repent—either in general, or of some particular wrong action you had forgotten.

As soon as your heart begins to have even one of these feelings, the pain immediately diminishes and the other two feelings can also come in. All these together will quickly establish such peace and good cheer within that you cannot help crying out: "Blessed be the name of the Lord forever!" The fact is that in a troubled heart these feelings are like oil on the waves of the sea: the waves are stilled and there is a great calm.

Therefore, bring peace to your heart—to whatever degree it may be troubled. And be assured: if by extended effort on yourself and by many spiritual labors you implant these feelings in your heart, so that it is always filled with them, then no affliction, distress, or hardship will ever trouble you. This attitude and frame of mind will stop them cold. I do not mean feelings of sorrow will never attack you. They will come, but will retreat at once—like waves from a strong and rock-hard cliff.

WHEN WE ARE WOUNDED IN WARFARE

Suppose you are wounded in your spiritual warfare: that is, you yield to some sin because of weakness or character fault. (I refer here to such milder sins as these: an inappropriate word slipped out, you lost your temper, a bad thought flashed in your head, an improper desire flared up, and so on.) Still, all is not lost. Remain calm; do not lose heart and fall into irrational confusion and anxiety.

Above all, don't dwell on yourself, saying, "How could I do that? How could I allow it? How could I be so stupid?" This sort of attitude is based on an exalted opinion of yourself. Rather, humble yourself, and raising your eyes to the Lord, say and feel, "What else could be expected of me, O Lord, weak and faulty as I am?"

Then go on to thank Him that the thing has gone no further, saying: "If it were not for Your unlimited mercy, O Lord, I would not have stopped at that, but would certainly have fallen into something far worse."

But you must not, along with this awareness and understanding of yourself, allow yourself to fall into the self-indulgent and careless thought that since you are weak, you have a right to behave wrongly—that it can't be helped. No, no! In spite of the fact that you are weak and imperfect, you are truly guilty for all the wrong things you do. Since you possess a will, all that comes forth from you is subject to that will. So in this sense, everything good counts in your favor and everything bad counts against you.

You are not chalking up points for and against yourself with God, of course, but you are revealing the state of your soul—and doing it good or evil. Therefore, conscious of your many sins and your tendency to fall into them, admit your guilt in the particular sin into which you have just fallen. Judge and condemn yourself, and only yourself.

Don't look around to see whom you can blame. Neither the people around you nor the circumstances are guilty of your sin. Your own disobedient will alone is to blame. So blame yourself.

Still, be careful. Don't imitate those who say: "Oh yes, I have done it. So what?" Don't just casually pass this sin off. Rather, having recognized your fault and reproached yourself, make yourself face the inescapable justice of God. Work quickly to warm up your feelings of contrition and remorse—not because of your own disgrace through sin, but because by your sin you have offended God. For He has shown you so much mercy in calling you to repentance, in remitting your past sins, in allowing you to participate in the grace of the Mysteries,[5] and in guiding and protecting your progress on the right path.

The deeper the contrition,[6] the better. However deep it may be, however, do not allow yourself a shadow of doubt about forgiveness. Forgiveness is already fully prepared and the record of all sins has been torn up on the cross (see Colossians 2:14). Repentance and contrition alone are expected of each of us before we can participate in the power of the redemption of the sins of the world through the Crucifixion. Therefore, trusting in this, prostrate yourself in soul and body, crying out to God: "Have mercy upon me, O God, according to Your lovingkindness" (Psalm 51:1). Keep on crying out until you feel yourself both guilty and forgiven—so guilt and forgiveness merge into one feeling.

The grace of this feeling finally comes to every repentant person—that is, to everyone who does as we have said above. But this must be accompanied by a firm decision and commitment not to indulge yourself in the future, but to guard and protect yourself from all downfalls, whether large or small. It must also be accompanied by a heartfelt prayer for the help of the grace of God in this undertaking.

After such a recent experience of the unreliability of our own powers and efforts, our heart will wish the help of God, as the psalmist says: "Create in me a clean heart, O God, and renew a steadfast spirit within me . . . Restore to me the joy of Your salvation, and uphold me with Your generous Spirit" (Psalm 51:10, 12).

All the above-mentioned things—self-condemnation, contrition, expectant prayer for forgiveness, the commitment to watch oneself in the future, prayer for help and for the gift of grace in this endeavor—all this, we must practice inwardly every time we commit sin with eyes, ears, tongue, thought, or feeling.

We must not, for a single moment, allow sin to remain in our heart unconfessed to the Lord and uncleansed by heartfelt repentance before Him. We may fall again, again and again, but each time we must repent. However often you sin, cleanse yourself each time before the Lord. Tell all to your spiritual guide (spiritual father or father confessor) as soon as possible. Such a confession of everything to our spiritual guide is very important in carrying on our spiritual warfare. [I know that some will say, "I do not know anyone who can be my spiritual father." Here is what to do in that case: Go to someone you trust and share your inner life with that person—man or woman. Then listen to what that friend tells you to do and do it.]

Nothing defeats our enemy's schemes and puts him to flight more effectively than this method of action. That is why the enemy tries every possible means, both inwardly and outwardly, to prevent our prompt repentance: inwardly by suggestions of thoughts and feelings; outwardly by arranging events, insofar as the Lord allows. Once you begin this work, you will discover what these obstacles are.

Just one warning, however: the enemy tries very hard to suggest you should not start on the work of your purification right away, when you first notice the sin. No, he will suggest, you should wait just a little while. Just as soon as you agree to this, however, he brings along another sin—after a sin with the tongue, perhaps one with the eyes, and then another with some other sense.

If you listen to him, you find yourself, without any particular qualms about it, postponing your purification of this second sin—since, after all, you must take care of the first one first. So on it goes, and you put off purification for a whole day, while sin after sin attacks your soul.

By evening, or perhaps bedtime, or even the end of the week, when you finally get around to working on purification by repentance, it has become very difficult to see clearly anything in your soul. Your soul is now filled with the noise, commotion, and darkness of the many trespasses you condoned in an offhand fashion by neglecting to deal with them.

In such cases our soul becomes like an eye blinded by dust particles, or like water muddied when dirt and filth have fallen into it. Since our soul can no longer see its condition, the work of repentance is abandoned altogether and the soul is left muddied, dirty, and clouded. So our prayers become imperfect, we are left unhappy and uncertain, and may even have bad dreams. Thus, a warning: never delay inner purification for even a single moment. As soon as you are aware of something wrong inside, deal with it.

One last thought: A common suggestion by the devil is that you should not tell your spiritual guide (spiritual father or father confessor) what has happened. Do not listen to that suggestion, but oppose it by disclosing everything to your guide. For just as this confession does us good, even more harm results from concealing what takes place in us and with us.

STUDY QUESTIONS

THE PROPER SCOPE OF SELF-DISTRUST
1. *Consider the good things set forth in the beginning of this section which can help us to do God's will—and the situations in which we may expect them to be helpful.*
2. *What must we do and keep on doing as long as life and breath shall last?*
3. *What should we do if we fail repeatedly and never seem to be able to do anything we believe is pleasing to God?*
4. *What can we say of the relation of God to His people in these situations and in all others? What hope do we have of victory?*

AVOID WORRYING AND A RESTLESS HEART

1. What have you been doing to overcome worries when they begin to get you down?
2. Can you make use of the ways recommended in this section to free yourself from sorrow, restlessness, and worries? Of what value to you are the general recommendations in the last part of the section?
3. How can we begin to make sure that future difficulties will not distract us from our trust in God and our relationship with Him?

WHEN WE ARE WOUNDED IN WARFARE

1. What do you do when you have sinned inadvertently? How does that differ from the recommendations given in this section?
2. Which of the recommendations in this section seem most applicable to you? How (if at all) can you make more of them applicable?
3. How does "keeping short accounts with God," as recommended in this section, relate to the maintenance of constant fellowship with Him?

CHAPTER 4

Satan's Master Battle Plan

TACTICS OF THE ENEMY

We must understand one thing above all about the devil: as far as we are concerned, all he cares about is to bring about our ruin. But he does not use the same tactics of warfare against everyone. To help understand this, let us look at some inner conditions people may have, the corresponding battle plans of the devil, and the means he uses to get around us and lure us into trouble.

A proper state of mind, soul, and body is one in which we have been freed from the chains of sin, are acquiring positive virtues, and are determined to remain upon that path. If we are not in this proper state—and are therefore vulnerable to the enemy—we may fall into one of the following categories:

• people remaining in the slavery of sin, having no thought of liberation from it;

• people under the slavery of sin who wish to be free, but do nothing to obtain freedom;

• people who have been freed from the chains of sin, and who have acquired virtues, but who once again fall into sin—with still greater moral corruption.

Further, in their self-delusion, some people in this third category think that, in spite of their sin, they are still advancing toward perfection; others thoughtlessly abandon the path of virtue; still others turn the very virtue they possess into a cause and means of harm for themselves.

As we shall see, the enemy influences each category of people in accordance with their condition and frame of mind.

HOW THE DEVIL KEEPS US SLAVES TO SIN

When the devil has managed to keep someone in slavery to sin, he takes special care to darken that person more and more by spiritual blindness—trying to keep out of his consciousness every good thought that might help him realize the poisoned condition of his life. He seeks to remove thoughts which could lead that person to repentance and the path of virtue. Then, at the same time, he replaces them with sinful and perverted thoughts. Along with such thoughts the enemy presents opportunities for committing the sin this person is most susceptible to, and entices him to fall into this, or even worse sins, as often as possible.

Thus, the poor sinner becomes progressively more blind and darkened. This blindness also strengthens the habit and impulse to go on constantly sinning. Consequently, led progressively from sinful action to greater blindness and from blindness to more and greater sins, the unhappy sinner whirls in this vortex. And he will continue to do so right up to death itself unless he forces himself to respond to the ever-present grace of God.

So, if we find ourselves in this dangerous condition and want to be freed from it, we must do the following:

• As soon as a good thought (or even a suggestion of

one) comes to you, calling you from darkness to light and from sin to virtue, immediately accept it wholeheartedly, with full attention and yearning.

• Then, diligently put that good thought into practice, calling from the bottom of your heart to the generous Giver of all blessings: "Help me, O Lord God, help me quickly, and do not let me remain in this sinful darkness." Never grow tired of appealing to God in these or similar words!

• At the same time, also look for help on earth, turning to those who know for advice and guidance on how to better free yourself from the bonds of sinful slavery which now hold you. If it is impossible to do this immediately, do so as soon as you get an opportunity.

• Also at the same time, keep on appealing to the Lord Jesus, who was crucified for you, asking Him to have mercy on you and never to deprive you of His help.

• Finally, realize that victory and triumph over the enemy can never be obtained by delaying, but only by readiness to rapidly follow an inner (or outer) prompt or reminder to truth, goodness, and righteousness.

ESCAPING FROM THE DEVIL'S NETS

Even after we have realized how dangerous and evil our sinful life is, it is still difficult to escape the devil's trickery. He attempts to keep us in his power, primarily by using a simple but all-powerful suggestion: "Later. Tomorrow. You can change later. You can do good tomorrow."

Deluded by the appearance of good intentions implied by this suggestion, we decide: "Sure. Tomorrow. Today I will take care of what I have to do. Then tomorrow, free of concern and worries, I will put myself in the hands of God's grace. Then I can follow the path of spiritual life without deviating to the right or to the left. So today I will take care of all these things. Tomorrow I will repent."

That is the trap with which the devil catches many people—and actually, in one sense, holds the whole world in his hands. But the real reason we are so easily caught in this trap is our own carelessness, laziness, and blindness.

Only these can explain why, when not only our own salvation, but the glory of God as well, are at stake, we fail to immediately use the easiest, simplest, yet most effective weapon—namely, to say to ourselves, with all determination and energy: "Right now! At this very moment and no later. I shall repent now instead of tomorrow. Now, this very moment is in my hands. Tomorrow and after are in the hands of God. Even if God grants me tomorrow and after, can I be sure that tomorrow I shall have this same good thought urging me to mend my ways?"

We all know that when we are offered a cure for an illness, it is stupid and foolish to say, "Wait! Let me be sick a little longer!" Anyone who delays the work of salvation does exactly that—with far more disastrous results.

So, if you want to be free of the delusion and deception of the enemy, if you want to overcome him, take up this trustworthy weapon against him at once. Obey—in actual deed—the good thoughts and promptings sent by the Lord, calling you to repent. Do not allow yourself the slightest delay, and don't permit yourself to say: "I have made a firm resolve to repent—but a little later—and I will not abandon that intent." That is one of the worst things you can do—and certainly the very worst at this time. Resolutions of this sort have always proven deceptive, and many people who relied on them have—for many reasons—remained unrepentant to the end of their lives. Among these reasons are:

• *Because our own resolutions are not based on distrust of our own abilities and a firm trust in God.* Consequently, we maintain a high opinion of ourselves—and one inescapable result of this is that, failing to accept divine help, we fall. That is why when we decide within, "Tomorrow I shall, without fail, abandon the path of sin," we always come up with the opposite: that is, instead of rising up, we fall down worse than before, and downfall after downfall follows.

God sometimes deliberately allows this to happen in order to bring self-reliant people to the realization of their own weakness—and to encourage them to seek divine help, renouncing and abandoning all trust in themselves, since only God's help can be trusted. When can we expect our own decisions to be steadfast and reliable? When we have abandoned all trust in ourselves, when all our hopes are based on humility and an unwavering trust in God alone.

• *When we make such resolutions, what we have in mind is the beauty and radiance of virtue—which do attract our will, no matter how weak and impotent it may be.* Today, as we make our resolution, the difficult side of virtue escapes our notice because the beauty of virtue is so attractive.

But tomorrow—ah, tomorrow—when our usual work and responsibilities must be faced, this attraction will not be nearly as strong, although we still remember our intention. As desire for this beauty weakens, our will also becomes weaker, or even relapses into its natural impotence. At the same time, the difficult side of virtue stands out and we see it for what it is—for the path of virtue, make no mistake, is hard by its very nature, and hardest of all at the first step.

Now, let us suppose that yesterday we decided to enter on this path, and we do so today. Strangely—but not so strangely—we no longer find any support from our will to carry out this decision. The desire has lost its intensity, our will has weakened, nothing but obstacles is in sight— obstacles within ourselves, in the habitual pattern of our life, in our usual relationships with others. So what do we decide? "I'll wait a while and gather my strength." So we go on waiting, from day to day, and it will be no wonder if we wait all our life!

If, on the other hand, we had started work yesterday, when the inspiring desire to mend our ways came upon us; if we had done something in obedience to this desire, if we had introduced into our life something in this spirit, today our desire and will would not be so weak as to retreat in the face of obstacles. Understand: there must be obstacles, but if we only had something to lean on within ourselves, we would overcome them, even if it were with difficulty. Had we given ourselves over all day to overcoming them, we would have felt them far less the next day—and on the third day, still less. Going further and further in that way we become established on the right path.

• *If we do not translate into practice the good intention of awakening from the sleep of sin, the awakening will not come so easily again.* Even if such awakenings do come, their effect on our will is not so strong as it was the first time. Our will is no longer as quick to incline toward following them, so even if the resolve to do so is there, it is now weak, lacking energy.

Consequently, if we are able to put off till tomorrow obedience to a strong impulse—and then lose that impulse altogether—it will be so much easier a second time and still more easy the third. And so it goes on: the more often we put off obedience to good impulses, the weaker their effect. After a time they lose their effect altogether, coming and going without a trace, and finally ceasing to come at all. We surrender ourselves to our downfall: our heart hardens and we begin to be actually hostile to good impulses. So delay becomes for us a straight road to final destruction—to hell itself.

Delays occur not only when we feel an inner impulse to exchange our bad life for a better, but also when we are already leading a good life. For instance, an opportunity presents itself to do good, and we put it off till tomorrow or till some other indefinite time. All we said about the first form of delay applies to this second kind as well—and it may indeed lead to the same consequences. If we miss a chance to do good, we not only deprive ourselves of the fruit of the good we might have done; we also offend God. Suppose, for instance, God sends us someone in need, and we say, "Go away. Come later." Although we say this to a human being, it is the same as saying it to God, who sent that person. God will find someone else to help that person, but we who refused will have to answer for it.

START OUT—AND WATCH OUT!

Suppose, however, that we have overcome the first two obstacles mentioned above, are filled with desire to be free of the bondage of sin, and have begun to work on it. Even then the enemy will not leave us alone.

He does change his tactics, but certainly not his evil desire—his hope to make us stumble against some stone of temptation and thus lead us to ruin. The Holy Fathers describe a person in this position as being under fire from all sides—from above and below, from left and right, from front and rear—from everywhere arrows come at us.

• Arrows from above are suggestions that we do spiritual work above our present abilities.

• Arrows from below are suggestions to reduce or even completely abandon all spiritual labors, through self-pity, carelessness, and thoughtlessness.

• Arrows come from the right when, in connection with some righteous undertaking, the devil and his allies lead us into temptation and danger of downfall.

• Arrows come from the left when those enemies present concrete temptations to draw us toward sin.

• Arrows come from the front when the devil and his agents tempt and disturb us by thoughts of what is to come.

• Arrows come from the rear when our enemies tempt us with memories of past acts and events.

All these tempting thoughts attack our soul either inwardly or outwardly. They attack inwardly through images and pictures of fantasy, mentally imprinted in our consciousness; or through direct evil suggestions planted in our heart, accompanied by impulses of passion generated from our own habits. They attack outwardly through the impressions received by the five external senses in a continuous flow.

Besides these, our enemies have allies in our former sinful habits and our own flesh, corrupted as it is by the fall of our race. Having so many means to harm us, the enemy is never discouraged by first failures. He simply and constantly puts into use now one, now another means of tripping or leading astray the servant of Christ who has avoided the previous attack.

After we have decided to abandon our wrong ways—and actually have abandoned them—the first undertaking of the enemy is to clear a space for an unhindered field of action against us. He often succeeds in this by suggesting to us, after we have set foot on the right path, that we should act on our own—instead of going for advice and guidance to the teachers of righteous life who are always to be found in connection with the Church.

If we follow their guidance and confirm our actions, both inner and outer, by the good judgment of our spiritual teachers (usually priests in our parishes, but other qualified spiritual teachers often rise up in the Church as well) there is no way the enemy can get to us. Whatever he may suggest, the experienced eyes of our spiritual teachers will at once see what he is driving at, and they will warn us. In that way the schemes of the enemy are defeated.

If we turn away from our spiritual teachers, the enemy can be counted on to confuse us and lead us astray. And remember, there are many things we can do which do not look evil to us, although their results may be evil—and these are the ones he suggests to us. The inexperienced disciple follows them and falls into an ambush, where he is exposed to great spiritual dangers or is even completely destroyed.

The second method used by the enemy is to lead an inexperienced disciple into a position in which he is not only without guidance, but without help. If we decide we can do without advice and guidance in our life, then left to ourselves we will soon come up with the idea that outside help is unnecessary for us to be able to live a righteous life and do good.

Unfortunately, however, the enemy is at work, speeding up our progress in coming to this notion. He conceals himself, refraining from attacking us during this time, so that, feeling free and unhampered, we begin to imagine that this seemingly good condition is the result of our own efforts. So we relax and continue to say our prayers for help from above, but now they are only mechanical—a meaningless formality. Since we are not really seeking help, none is given, so we, inexperienced and self-trusting disciples, are left to our own devices and powers. That is when we are easy prey for the enemy.

The results of this self-deception are varied. In some cases people undertake spiritual exercises and works that are both untimely and beyond their powers. At first the strong burst of energy produced by self-reliance gives them the strength to sustain such works—but this is only for a while. Soon the strength of most people is exhausted and they barely find energy to make the most moderate efforts. Often they abandon their efforts completely.

Some people, however, firing up their self-willed energy more and more, reach such a degree of self-reliance that they end up believing they can do anything. In this state of delirium they take disastrous steps: stop eating altogether, throw themselves from high places, and the like. And remember, all this, unbeknown to the tempted person, is arranged by the enemy.

Another result of self-deception and of ascribing one's successes to oneself is appropriating the right to give oneself special dispensations and indulgences. There is a form of delusion which, when something new is introduced into life such as repentance, makes days seem like months and weeks like years.

Thus, if we have made a few efforts in the new order of life, the enemy hammers into our head the illusion: "I have worked so hard, have fasted so long, spent so many nights without sleep and so on. It's time for a rest." "Rest a while," the enemy suggests, "give the flesh a break. It's time for a little amusement." Then, just as soon as the inexperienced beginner agrees to this, indulgence follows indulgence till the whole order of righteous life is upset. Back we drop into the life we had abandoned, beginning to live carelessly and thoughtlessly, never rolling up our sleeves.

Temptations of this sort—to avoid the advice and guidance of others, to ascribe successes to oneself, to undertake excessive works, or to give oneself dispensations—are used by the devil not just at the beginning of righteous life. He attempts to use these suggestions throughout its whole course. So we see how important it is for us to do everything under guidance; never to ascribe any successes, however small, to ourselves, to our own powers and our own zeal; to avoid all excesses and indulgences; and to lead a life which, though balanced, is energetic and alive. We should always follow the order and rule already established by the example of the saints who lived before us, and by the good judgment of experienced men and women who are our contemporaries.

STUDY QUESTIONS

TACTICS OF THE ENEMY
1. *Consider the descriptions of different spiritual conditions given at the beginning of the chapter. Keeping in mind that we cannot accurately judge our own condition without the help of our spiritual father, do you have an idea into which of these categories you might fall?*

HOW THE DEVIL KEEPS US SLAVES TO SIN
1. *What experiences have you had in fighting the devil's tactics to keep you in slavery to sin?*
2. *Consider the recommendations for getting free of this slavery. How would you suggest implementing these recommendations?*

ESCAPING FROM THE DEVIL'S NETS
1. *Have you ever been trapped by the "good-intentions-for-tomorrow" tactic? How did you escape?*
2. *Consider the reasons given for failing to deal promptly and thoroughly with our sin. Does one of them especially stand*

out as an obstacle to your own spiritual growth? How do you fight it?

START OUT—AND WATCH OUT!

1. *Consider the various directions of attack our spiritual fathers tell us to expect from the devil and his angels. Which of them have you experienced? How have these attacks affected your efforts in building your inner life?*
2. *Note the first method used by the enemy to steer us away from the right path. What experience have you had with this?*
3. *Have you been in a position to be attacked by the second method of deception? What did you do to escape?*
4. *Which of the results of self-deception have troubled you most?*

scripture
fellowship;
Prayer.

CHAPTER 5

Lessons from Life

FORGET HARDSHIPS AND DO GOD'S WILL

If we are enduring some hardship with a thankful heart, we must pay attention lest our enemy succeed in tempting us, or our self-love build up a desire to be rid of the hardship. For if that happens, we will suffer a double loss:

• Although the appearance of such a desire (and our consent to it) does not immediately rob us of the virtue of patience, it does greatly undermine it. Then when our desire to be free of our hardship or difficulty is not fulfilled, our patience gradually weakens. Eventually, impatience rules.

• From the moment we entertain such a desire, our patience becomes forced and artificial, whereas God loves and rewards what is given freely. Therefore, from that moment on, although we must still bear the same hardships and difficulties (for just wanting to be free of them does not get rid of them), our endurance will be unrewarded. God will reward us for enduring our afflictions when we endure them with a good spirit and a good attitude. But from the moment we decide we wish to be free of them, a change takes place: God does not reward unwilling endurance.

If, on the other hand, we squelch and reject the desire

to be free from troubles and hardships just as soon as it rears its ugly head, throwing ourselves completely on the compassionate will of God, declaring our readiness to suffer even a hundred times greater sorrows if God wishes to send them, then, even if our present tribulation lasts only an hour (or even less), God will accept it as if it were of the longest possible duration and reward us accordingly.

We must learn to treat all other situations in the same manner, not knuckling under to our desires, but keeping a tight rein on them, directing them to the one primary aim: to stay within the will of God and to do His will. If we do that, our desires will turn around, becoming good and righteous. We will stay calm in every storm, finding peace in God's will. In fact, if we sincerely believe that nothing can happen to us except by His will—and if we have no other desire than to be actively doing that will—it is self-evident that we will always get only what we desire!

Of course, when I say nothing can happen to you except by God's will, I am referring to the hardships, difficulties, and losses God sends to reprove and teach us or to punish us for our sins. I am not referring to our own or other people's sins themselves, for God does not want anyone to sin. The trials He sends are beneficial to us and are sometimes accurately called "a saving cross," which He often imposes on those who love Him most and try to please Him. He is especially pleased when we bear our crosses.

When we wrote above that we should not desire to be free of afflictions, we meant that we should always be submissive to God's will. We cannot help wishing to be free of misfortune, for God Himself made the desire for well-being a part of our nature. In fact, He Himself taught us to make the request, "Lead us not into temptation"—a prayer we repeat several times a day!

But if, after we pray this prayer (which God is sure to hear), He sends us trouble, it is clearly His specific will—to which we, as His creatures, conscious of our duty to obey Him in everything, should submit with a good spirit, enduring our trial as something essential to our salvation.

In addition, when we pray, "Lead us not into temptation," we must maintain the attitude, "Nevertheless, not as I will, but as You will" (Matthew 26:39)—in imitation of our Savior. In other words, we say this prayer not because we abhor temptations so much we want to avoid them at all costs, but because the Lord commanded us to pray it. His desire is that we keep within our soul a total readiness to accept with a good spirit all God pleases to send us, refusing to pander to the self-loving desire for uninterrupted well-being—which is impossible on earth anyway, since it belongs to the future eternal life.

WATCH OUT FOR DECEIT

When the devil, deceitful as he is, sees us moving along properly on the path of virtue in spite of his attempts to lead us astray by his obvious temptations to sin, he changes his tactics. Transforming himself into an angel of light, he suggests the following things, as they suit his purposes: apparently good thoughts, texts from the Holy Scriptures, and examples of the saints. Through all these he attempts to persuade us to make extreme, unreasonable, and untimely efforts at spiritual perfection. For his aim, we remember, is to cast us down into the abyss at the moment we imagine we stand on the summit.

This is why he teaches some people to torment their flesh by excessive fasting and other bodily hardships—in order to make them fall into pride, imagining they are achieving great things. Or he makes them fall ill from extreme exhaustion so they become incapable of performing even the smallest righteous deeds. Or he makes them so tired of the burden of their efforts that they become indifferent to all spiritual endeavor, and even to salvation itself—and then, with their enthusiasm for good growing gradually cooler, they throw themselves into the lusts of the flesh and worldly comforts with more gusto than before.

We can never know how many souls have fallen into this snare of the devil—carried away by the intensity of their foolish zeal, in their excessive discipline of their bodies going beyond what they are able to bear, suffering in self-torment of their own invention, and becoming the laughingstock of evil demons! Note that this would never have happened if they had followed good judgment and advice, and had not forgotten that bodily discipline, though admirable and fruitful where there is sufficient strength of the body and humility of the soul, must always be controlled by good sense and used only as a means to spiritual progress.

The discipline of the body must never become an aim in itself, and indeed ascetic practices must sometimes be reduced, sometimes increased, sometimes changed, and sometimes stopped altogether for a time.

Those who cannot be as strict with themselves as some of the saints—nor carry out as strong ascetic practices—can imitate their lives in other ways. They can arouse and establish good dispositions in their hearts, acquire the habit of fervent prayer, wage unrelenting war against thoughts and desires inspired by the passions, protect the purity of their hearts, love silence and solitude, be humble and meek with all people, do good to those who have caused them suffering, and guard themselves against all evil, however insignificant.

All these righteous activities of heart are more pleasing to God than excessive accomplishments of subduing, controlling, and putting down the flesh—especially when the latter are not required by our moral condition.

We must use good judgment in undertaking tasks of physical asceticism when they are needed for our spiritual gain.

First, avoid launching out with lofty standards, but rather begin at the bottom. It is better to climb up gradually than to suddenly undertake something lofty and be forced to climb down to a more realistic level (to your shame).

At the same time, also avoid the other extreme, into which even people who are considered very spiritual sometimes fall. Under the influence of self-pity and self-indulgence, they exhibit too great a concern for the preservation of their physical health—taking such great care of themselves that they tremble at the slightest physical effort, for fear of impairing their health.

Such people cannot think or talk about anything else than preserving their life. At the same time, by inventing delicate dishes which cater more to their refined tastes than does simple, healthy food, they actually weaken and even impair their health. And this is not even to mention that they are, in the process, depriving themselves of the very blessings they prize so highly because they are unable or unwilling to do what is necessary to attain them.

Although these people justify their very dissimilar actions by desire to work for the Lord, they are actually attempting to reconcile two irreconcilable enemies: flesh and spirit. These efforts not only fail to benefit either flesh or spirit, but actually work obvious harm to both alike, for they deprive body and spirit of health.

We simply must recognize that a moderate and orderly way of life, controlled by reason, taking account of the needs of the soul and the particular condition of the body, is much less dangerous and certainly more useful for both the soul and the body. In this respect the standard is not the same for everyone, but one rule does apply to all of us: to keep the body submissive to the spirit.

Finally, we must also remember something said earlier: The acquisition of virtues, whether of the body or of the soul, should be gradual, climbing up little by little.

HOW TO STOP JUDGING OTHERS

Our self-love and high opinion of ourselves give birth within us to yet another sin which damages us greatly. That sin is severe judgment and condemnation of our neighbors—demonstrated when we consider them of little or no value, despise them, and (when opportunity arises) humiliate them.

This sinful habit, born of pride, feeds and grows on pride—and in turn feeds pride and makes it grow. Every time we pass judgment, our pride grows a bit more because of the accompanying feelings of self-importance and self-gratification.

Since we value (and think of) ourselves so highly, we naturally look at others as if from on high (as if from a judgment seat), judging and despising them. For we seem to exempt ourselves from those faults we think others possess. Right there our enemy, the devil, who constantly looks for an opportunity to damage us, finds an opening. Seeing our sinful state of spirit and heart, he suggests we keep a sharp watch on what others say and do. And he leads us to draw conclusions from these observations concerning what others think and feel. Then, on the basis of these suppositions, we form an opinion of them (generally not good), exaggerating this supposed fault until we conclude that the person we are judging has a deeply rooted character defect.

Alas! When we so judge others, we neither see nor realize that the very origin of our judgment—the suspicion of wrong on the part of others—is actually planted in our mind by the action of our enemy. Nor do we even suspect that he is behind our thoughts, fanning this suspicion into a certainty that the people we judge are as we imagine them to be—even though they are not.

Therefore we must keep a sharp lookout. The enemy watches us constantly, waiting for an opportunity to sow evil in us. So we must keep an ever-increasing watch over ourselves, lest we fall into the trap he sets for us. Just as soon as he shows us some fault in our neighbor, we must quickly reject the thought—lest it take root in us and grow. Take warning: we must cast it out so no trace is left in us, and replace it with thoughts of the good qualities we know our neighbor possesses (or of those qualities people generally should possess).

Then, if we still feel the impulse to pass judgment, let us add to these thoughts this fact: We are given no authority to pass judgment, and the moment we assume this authority we make ourselves worthy of judgment and condemnation—not before powerless people, but before God, the all-powerful Judge of all!

This reversal of attitudes is one of the best and strongest means not only of rejecting stray critical thoughts that pop into our minds, but also (with constant attention and much work) of freeing ourselves from this sin.

The second method, equally strong (and equally difficult!), is never to let ourselves forget our own wickedness, our polluted and sinful passions and behavior—and correspondingly to hold on to the constant realization of our own unworthiness. We will certainly find in ourselves many such passions—as well as the behavior they inspire!

If we have not finally given up and shrugged our shoulders, saying, "Whatever will be, will be," we cannot help wanting to find a cure for these diseases, which are truly killing us more surely than any physical ailment. And we can be sure of this: if we sincerely devote ourselves to this work, we will have no time to concern ourselves with the affairs of others or to pass sentence on them. For once we go at it, there will ring in our ears sayings such as:

"Physician, heal yourself!" (Luke 4:23), and "First remove the plank from your own eye" (Matthew 7:5).

Furthermore, when we severely judge some wrong behavior on the part of our neighbor, we must realize that there is (at least) a small root of the same sin lying within our own heart—which, through its relation to our passions, tells us to make assumptions about others and to judge them. We know that "an evil man out of the evil treasure [of his heart] brings forth evil things" (Matthew 12:35). But an eye that is pure and not under the influence of sinful passions also looks on the behavior of others without passion—and without evil.

We recall the words of Scripture, "You are of purer eyes than to behold evil, and cannot look on wickedness" (Habakkuk 1:13). When, therefore, the thought enters our mind to condemn someone for some fault, we must turn it around and be indignant with ourselves for committing the same actions—being guilty of the same fault. Then, in our hearts let us say: "How can I, unworthy as I am, lift up my head to look at the faults of others and condemn them, when I am immersed in the same sin and my own trespasses are even greater?" By doing this we turn against ourselves that weapon which our evil thought urges us to use against someone else—and instead of wounding our brother or sister, we will give first aid, at least, to our own wounds.

If the sin of your neighbor is not hidden but obvious to everyone, try to see its cause—not in the way the wicked passion for judging suggests, but as a Christian brother or sister should see it. Say to yourself: "Since this neighbor of mine has many hidden virtues, God has allowed him to fall into this present sin in order to protect him from being damaged by conceit and pride. Or He has allowed this person to take on this very unbecoming appearance so that he will appear unworthy in his own eyes—and being despised by others for being in this condition, he will gather the fruits of humility and become even more pleasing to God." In this way we will believe that the present instance of sin will do our neighbor more good than harm.

And even if a person's sin is not only obvious, but very serious, and comes from a hardened and unrepentant heart, let us not condemn him. Rather, we must lift up our eyes to the wonderful and incomprehensible judgments of God. Then we will see that many people who were once filled with iniquity have later repented and reached a high degree of holiness. Others, on the other hand, who were once on a high level of perfection, have fallen into a deep chasm. Let us take care lest we also suffer such a calamity through judging others.

Therefore, we must always be on guard in fear and trembling—fearing more for ourselves than for others. Further, we may be assured that every good word we utter on behalf of our neighbor, and every rejoicing for his sake, is the action and fruit of the Holy Spirit within us. On the other hand, every bad word and scornful condemnation comes from our own sinful tendencies and the suggestions of the devil. Therefore, when we are tempted by some wrong behavior on the part of our neighbor, let us not sleep until we have driven this temptation from our heart—and completely made peace with our brother or sister.

SURRENDERING OURSELVES TO GOD'S WILL

When someone has repented, he gives himself up to the service of God, and immediately begins this service by obeying His commandments and His will. The fact is that this work, this labor, begins with the sweat of the brow. Commandments are not hard in themselves, but there are many obstacles to practicing them when we begin to apply them to our own external circumstances—and especially to our inner tendencies and habits. But with God's help a tireless fighter overcomes everything in the end, achieving peace within and a calm flow of events on the outside (relatively, of course).

The one who struggles always acts—but with the help of God. The experience of his first days of struggle makes him realize that in spite of all his efforts, if anything good is accomplished, it is done only because he is given power from on high to do it. The further he goes, the more this conviction grows and the more deeply rooted it becomes. When comparative peace within is established, this conviction is emphasized and takes command, finally resulting in complete submission to God's will and total surrender to His influence.

In those who struggle for salvation, God's influence begins to act from the very first moments of their turning to Him—and, in fact, brings about the turning itself. But it begins to grow as the struggler turns further and further away from himself, attaching himself to God, and as, realizing his own inability, he builds a growing trust in God's power. When he finally surrenders himself entirely to God, God is actively present in him—both in showing what he must do and in fulfilling it.

This is the ultimate, the summit, if you will, of Christian perfection, in which "it is God who works in you both to will and to do for His good pleasure" (Philippians 2:13). As we noted at the start, the seed of this perfection lies in learning not to rely on ourselves, but to hope in God—and here it is shown in full maturity.

What makes up the essence of total submission to the will of God can be seen when it is demonstrated to the fullest extent. There are no special rules for acquiring it, for it comes as we give ourselves over to Him—so it is impossible to say, "Do this and you will receive it." Total surrender to God grows imperceptibly as we turn from reliance on ourselves to hope in God.

We reach that state of total submission as we gradually die to ourselves—that is, to our own opinions, wishes, feelings, and tastes, in order to live by divine guidance. This we obtain by conforming ourselves with God's will and partaking of Him (see 2 Peter 1:4). In the forefront of all this endeavor is our Lord and Savior. He surrendered the whole of Himself to God the Father—and us in Himself, for as the Apostle Paul writes: "We are members of His body, of His flesh and of His bones" (Ephesians 5:30).

Our Lord Jesus prayed to God the Father for us: "And for their sakes I sanctify Myself, that they also may be sanctified by the truth" (John 17:19). Let us share with Him in the hope that we shall indeed be sanctified, and behave as those who are. Total surrender of the will to God is actually the sacrificing of oneself as a burnt offering (so to speak) to God.

Why is this sacrifice of ourselves made at the end of our journey instead of at the beginning? Because an offering to God must be perfect, without blemish. In the beginning we seek perfection, but we have not yet attained it. When in the end it is finally attained, then it is fitting to offer ourselves as a sacrifice. At first one only dedicates himself to this sacrifice, but at the end he actually makes the sacrifice of himself.

It is impossible to sacrifice oneself as a burnt offering before attaining perfection. Other sacrifices can be offered, such as thanksgiving offerings and offerings of purification, but not the burnt offering. We can attempt it and we can talk about it, but it will simply be words and not the actual deed—which is ultimately accomplished without words.

We must understand that as long as we are still attached to anything earthly, as long as we lean on anything within or without that is not God, as long as we find our enjoyment in something created, we are unfit to be a burnt offering. We must come to the point of endeavoring to renounce all this, making all the lives inside us stop, with only one life remaining—life in God. In other words, we must come to the point at which we no longer live, but instead God the Father, our Lord Jesus Christ, and the Holy Spirit live in us (see Galatians 2:20).

When you have reached that point, sacrifice yourself to God—or rather, you will be sacrificed to God. Until this time comes, have as an offering to God a contrite spirit, and a contrite and humble heart. Be content with this for a time, but not forever. In the end you must come to the point of sacrificing yourself completely as a burnt offering to God.

STUDY QUESTIONS

FORGET HARDSHIPS AND DO GOD'S WILL

1. *How can we accept hardship as a gift of God and live with it patiently and with a good spirit?*
2. *What is the central lesson of this section? How can you apply it to the current conditions under which you live?*

WATCH OUT FOR DECEIT

1. *What do you consider to be the greatest danger to you in the matters discussed in this section?*
2. *How can we avoid going beyond our ability in our zeal for spiritual progress? What have you done to help guide yourself in this aspect of spiritual warfare?*

HOW TO STOP JUDGING OTHERS

1. *What adverse outcomes have you seen from judging others severely?*
2. *Do you often find yourself making severe judgments of other people? If so, how do you overcome this tendency?*
3. *How can the suggestions given in this section be adapted to help you avoid severe judgments of other people?*

SURRENDERING OURSELVES TO GOD'S WILL

1. *What experience of surrendering yourself to the will of God have you had in the past?*
2. *What do you see as the most important element in our surrender of ourselves to God?*
3. *How, following the advice of this section, would you, in turn, advise someone to go about that surrender?*

CHAPTER 6

Warmth of Heart
and Purity of Conscience

WARMING A COLD, DRY HEART

Spiritual warmth of heart is the fruit of yearning for God and everything pertaining to Him. This warmth is actually born when we turn to God in repentance. In the course of our efforts to purify our heart, the warmth gains more and more strength, so that we rise gradually from intermittent feelings of warmth in our heart to a more constant warming, until finally warmth becomes, by God's grace, a permanent state.

In one place in his writings Saint John of the Ladder advised: "Strive always to have feelings toward God and divine things." He meant that we should strive to have this warmth.

Every object which delights the heart warms it, so warmth of heart can be of many kinds. Spiritual warmth is born through the influence of spiritual things upon the heart, which is built up through the progress of our spiritual life. Its distinctive feature is renunciation of all created things, which occurs when the attention is totally captivated by God and by everything godly and heavenly. Therefore it is as far removed from mere warm feelings of soul and body as heaven is removed from earth.

The feeling of spiritual warmth is concentrated and

seems uncomplicated and specific. In its essence, however, it is a fusion of many spiritual operations—just as a ray of light is the fusion of all the colors of the spectrum. It contains (at least) these elements: reverence, contrition, tenderness, prostrating oneself before God, worship, holy zeal, and love of God.

Since these spiritual feelings cannot all become established at once, spiritual warmth does not instantly become an attribute of our heart.

Until spiritual warmth of heart has become a permanent condition, it comes and goes. Either it comes on its own, as a heavenly guest, or it is a fruit of spiritual exercises—such as reading, meditation, prayer, acts of self-denial, and good works. It leaves when attention strays from spiritual subjects, following which the heart partakes of things not of the spirit and delights in them. This quenches spiritual warmth, just as water quenches fire.

But suppose we want to preserve this spiritual warmth in our heart. What do we do? Just this:

• Maintain our attention within and stand praying in our hearts before God.

• Do not allow our thoughts to wander, distracting our attention.

• Let no sympathy for things of either the soul or the body enter our heart.

• Cut off all cares and worries at their onset.

• Keep alive our zeal to please God and to save our souls.

• In all external affairs, follow the order dictated by reason, directing them all toward our chief aim.

Conceptelin on the Lord.

• While doing one thing, we must not burden our thoughts by cares about the many.

At the same time we must add that once we have experienced this spiritual warmth, we cannot help endeavoring to keep it. In doing so, we must use proper means. If we do, we will discover the best way to keep it. If we carry this out with good judgment, spiritual warmth will become our trustworthy guide, teaching us how to control our inner life, how to behave in external affairs, and how to control our conduct in order to keep this very thing.

Just as the presence of spiritual warmth in the heart is sweet, its absence is correspondingly bitter, wearisome, and frightening. We have already noted that it goes away when the attention and the heart stray from the things of the spirit, turning toward things not of the spirit. We are not referring here to sinful things; a person who has had a taste of spiritual warmth is no longer attracted by sin. We simply mean anything belonging to the soul-body realm—anything pointless, earthly, created.

As soon as attention inclines toward such things, spiritual warmth immediately declines. And when the heart also turns that way and adheres to any such thing, spiritual warmth withdraws entirely—leaving behind coldness toward all things godly and toward God Himself, accompanied by indifference to all spiritual works and activities practiced for the purpose of preserving this warmth.

If a person in such circumstances remembers right away what he is about and hastens to reestablish his customary, warmth-producing pattern of life, this warmth returns—sometimes slowly, sometimes quickly. But if he pays no attention to it and, through becoming scattered, infatuated with something, or self-reliant, deliberately allows himself to linger in this cooling atmosphere (and especially if he takes the risk of satisfying in actual behavior his nonspiritual tastes which have been resurrected by it), his very zeal for spiritual life is undermined—if not completely deadened.

This latter condition is the forerunner of falling into his once-habitual sins—a fate which will surely overtake a careless person. But if such a person remembers what he is about and where he is headed, he can return without too much difficulty, even from there, to his previous good spiritual condition.

The above process is how spiritual cooling always happens. It comes about through our own fault, since it is caused by a decrease in attention and watchfulness over ourselves. This diminution of our attention comes about either as a response to the temptations existing in our surroundings—when various kinds of worldly delusion blunt and captivate us—or by the wiles of the enemy, who manages to persuade us to come out of our inner self.

The enemy sometimes manages to do this merely by inserting his own more attractive pictures in the natural flow of images of fantasy—and sometimes by affecting the body in some way. But whatever the cause, cooling begins with our attention straying from our inner depths. It makes further progress when our heart attaches itself to something pointless and empty, which leads in turn (if unchecked) to excitement by sinful passions. In every case it is our own fault. For we must always remember this—

neither the world nor the devil can violate our freedom; they can only subject us to temptation.

Sometimes cooling comes about through the action of grace. Examined from the correct perspective, spiritual warmth must be seen as the fruit of grace present in the heart. When grace comes, the heart is warm. When grace goes, the heart is cold. Grace also leaves us when we deviate from attention to our inner selves because we are attracted by wrong things. Then the cooling can be called punitive.

Sometimes, however, grace is withdrawn for the purpose of assisting the spiritual progress of the servants of God. When that happens, the cooling can be called instructive. The consequences, however, are still the same: cooling and a sensation of emptiness in the heart, for the guest and visitor has gone.

The difference between these coolings is that the guilty cooling weakens even our desire for spiritual life. Cooling due to an instructive withdrawal of grace, however, makes that desire burn with even greater fervor—which is one of the purposes of such withdrawal.

Divine grace may be withdrawn for several different instructional purposes:

• To stimulate zeal, which sometimes slackens during a long period of calm.

• To make us examine our situation with greater attention and reject those attachments and activities not directly connected with a life acceptable to God and not leading to Him.

• To increase and strengthen the consciousness and feeling that everything good in us is the fruit of God's grace.

• To make us value the gifts of God more highly in the future, care more about preserving them, and be more deeply humble.

• To make us surrender ourselves with greater sincerity to the hands of divine Providence—with complete self-denial and self-minimization.

• To force us not to become attached to spiritual delights in and of themselves, thus dividing our heart—for God wishes the whole of it to belong to Him alone.

• To prevent us from relaxing our efforts when divine grace works in us, and instead to make us work without sleeping on the path of God—exerting all the powers He has given us especially for this purpose.

Consequently, we see that even when spiritual cooling results from an instructive withdrawal of divine grace, we ourselves are the cause of it. For although divine grace withdraws of its own accord, it does so because we need this discipline.

ENDURING COOLNESS WITH PATIENCE

So when you feel a cooling of your desire for spiritual things and activities, and for all things holy and sacred in general, look deeply within yourself and carefully examine what has happened. If it is your fault, go to work quickly to eliminate that fault and destroy it—not so much because you are anxious for the return of spiritual blessings, but rather because you want to destroy in yourself everything inappropriate and not pleasing to God.

If, on the other hand, we examine ourselves and find nothing unsuitable or displeasing to God, the proper thing to do is simply to submit to God's will, saying to ourselves: "God has decided this is the way it is to be for now. Let Your will be done in me, O Lord, weak and unworthy as I am."

Then we must be patient and wait, never allowing ourselves to depart from the customary order of our spiritual life, spiritual works and exercises. Along with this, let us overcome any lack of taste for these efforts which may have attacked us—by forcing ourselves to practice them, paying no attention to thoughts which try to distract us from our efforts by suggesting that all this is useless. And let us willingly drink our cup of bitterness, saying to the Lord: "See my humility and my efforts, O Lord, and do not deprive me of Your mercy."

Then, let our efforts be stimulated by the faith that this cup comes from God's love for us—for He desires us to attain to greater spiritual perfection.

We must, then, follow in the footsteps of the Lord—not only to Mount Tabor (where He was transfigured), but also to Golgotha (where He was crucified). In other words, we must simply follow Him: not only when we feel divine light and spiritual joys and blessings within, but also when we are attacked by darkness, tribulations, stress, and bitterness. Our soul has to experience these things at times from the temptations of the demons—within and without.

Even if this cooling is accompanied by such darkness and confusion that we do not know what to do or where to turn, we are to have no fear. Instead, let us stand firm, remain submissively on our cross, and cast far away from us every earthly comfort which the world and the flesh choose to offer, prompted by the enemy.

Further, we must also try to hide our sickness from all other people, speaking of it to no one but our spiritual father. Nor is it proper for us to complain about the spiritual tribulation we are undergoing; rather we should seek guidance on how to avoid it in the future, and how to suffer it with a good heart and attitude now—for as long as God pleases to keep us in it.

In the meantime, let us continue to practice our prayers, Communion, and other spiritual exercises just as usual—not for the sake of spiritual blessings, nor in order to be taken down from our present cross, but so that we may be given strength to remain nailed to that cross with our soul undisturbed, to the glory of Christ our Lord, who was crucified for us, and to always live and behave in a way pleasing to Him.

If our condition sometimes makes it impossible for us to pray and to have good thoughts as before—because of great darkness and confusion in our spirit—we must simply do the best we can, as long as we do so without laziness or self-indulgence. Then the lack of perfection in execution will be accepted as perfect for the sake of our desire, effort, and seeking. If we continue with that desire, effort, and seeking, we will see its wonderful fruits—inspiration and strength filling our soul.

We can find in the Scriptures excellent examples of how to call to God in such times of darkening of our spirit. We can call out: "Why are you cast down, O my soul? And why are you disquieted within me? Hope in God; for I shall yet praise Him, the help of my countenance and my God" (Psalm 43:5).

And, "Why do You stand afar off, O Lord? Why do You hide in times of [my] trouble?" (Psalm 10:1).

And further: "Do not forsake me, O LORD; O my God, be not far from me!" (Psalm 38:21).

Remembering how Sarah, the beloved wife of Tobias, was inspired by God to pray in her trouble (Tobit 3:11-15), cry out: "Everyone who works for You, O Lord, truly knows that if this life is a trial, it will be crowned, and if it is filled with afflictions, it will be redeemed and, by Your mercy, will not cease even in corruption. You do not rejoice in our destruction, but bring calm after storm and joy after tears and weeping. Blessed be Your name forever, O God of Israel!"

It is also proper to bring to our recollection Christ our Lord, who, through His immeasurable sufferings, felt Himself abandoned by His heavenly Father in the garden of Gethsemane and on the cross. And when we feel as if we are crucified in our present position, let us cry out from our heart, "Your will be done, O Lord!" and "Not as I will, but as You will" (Matthew 26:39).

If we do this, our patience and our prayer will rise on high to God's presence, as the flame of the sacrifice of our heart. And we will prove ourselves filled with love as strong as death, as well as fervent readiness of will to shoulder our cross and follow Christ our Lord on any path by which He chooses to call us to Himself. This is true life in God: to desire and seek God for His own sake, and to possess Him and partake of Him in the way and to the extent He wishes.

If we entered the path of godly life with this attitude and measured our progress by its strength (instead of by the shifting tides of spiritual joys and blessings), we would not be so easily overcome by temptations which come on their own or through the wiles of the enemy, nor would we uselessly grieve or complain when times of cooling and dryness come.

On the contrary, we would accept such times thankfully and endure them gladly, convinced that if it is God's will, it must be for our own good. Disregarding them, we would continue along the path of a life pleasing to God, observing all the commandments with still greater zeal, greater self-denial, and greater exertion.

It sometimes happens that while the soul goes along despairing in this state of coolness of spiritual fervor and absence of taste for anything spiritual, the enemy attacks with greater force, arousing evil thoughts, shameful impulses, and seductive dreams. His aim is to provoke hopelessness through the sense of being abandoned by God, and to make us give up the struggle. He aims to bend us toward some act of the passions so he can easily lead us back into the whirlpool of sinful life.

Being aware of this, we must stand firm. So what if waves of sin roar around our heart? Just so long as our heart is filled with hostility to sin and with desire to be faithful to God, our little boat is safe. Divine grace has withdrawn its comforts from us, but it stands nearby, watching. It will not leave us without help as long as our will is on the side of good.

Again, we must stand firm, motivated by the certainty that this storm will soon be over and with it our spiritual dryness will leave. We must also believe this is allowed for our own good. For, if we endure this time of trial and temptation, we will come out of it with greater knowledge of our own weakness, greater humility, and a stronger conviction that God's help is always ready at hand.

In previous chapters we have written of such tempestuous attacks by the enemy. It will do us all good to review these chapters once more!

GUARDING OUR CONSCIENCE

We must use every possible means to keep our conscience pure, keeping it blameless in thoughts, words, and deeds, and never letting it reproach us and gnaw at us for anything.

If we do this, we will gain strength in both our inner and outer behavior. Ruling all aspects of our life, we will govern it appropriately. A pure conscience will make our life blameless, for it will be sensitive and strong for good against evil. Conscience is the law inscribed by God in the hearts of people to shed light on their path and guide them in righteousness, as the Apostle Paul teaches, calling it, "the work of the law written in their hearts" (Romans 2:15). On the basis of this, Saint Nilus (of Sinai, died c. 450) gives the following advice: "In all your works follow the guidance of conscience like a lamp."

There are four relationships in which we must keep our conscience blameless. The first is in relation to God. The second is in relation to ourselves. The third is in relation to our neighbors. And the fourth is in relation to everything in our possession.

This is, of course, nothing new, but there are certain

points about each we need to keep in mind.

In relation to God you must do these things:

• Abide in remembrance of God and walk in His presence.

• Be aware of being personally carried and protected by God, and led toward the goal for which He called you into existence.

• Dedicate yourself and all you have to the service of God and the glory of His name.

• Live in God, have trust in Him, and surrender your fate to Him—both in time and in eternity.

In relation to yourself, these actions are necessary:

• Let your spirit, which seeks the heavenly and eternal God, rule over your soul and body, whose joint function is to organize our temporal life.

• Let your soul obey the guidance of your spirit, and bow the neck of your spirit to truth revealed by God, which will illumine the whole scope of its knowledge.

• Let your spirit keep your will attuned to the commandments of God, not allowing it to turn aside toward its own desire, in opposition to them.

• Let your spirit teach your heart to find value only in divine matters and in those things which bear the imprint of God and are its expression.

• In this same manner, let your spirit order and conduct your affairs, both public and those of daily life.

• Give your body what it needs, observing strict allowances, and establish for yourself the rule to "make no provision for the flesh, to fulfill its lusts" (Romans 13:14)—ever, in anything. If you keep to this, you will be a good ruler and benefactor of yourself.

In relation to your neighbors, observe the following:

• Respect them all as being images of God.

• Wish them all well and do good to them as much as you are able.

• Be humble before everyone and seek to please them all within the limits of what is good.

• Rejoice with those who rejoice, and grieve with those who grieve.

• Do not judge or humiliate anyone, even in thought or feeling.

• Do not conceal the truth (if you know it) from those who seek guidance and advice from you; however, do not impose yourself upon anyone as a teacher of your own accord.

• Above all, keep peace and harmony with everyone, being ready on your part to make any sacrifice to do this. Take every care to lead no one astray.

In relation to material things, act in this manner:

• Respect all things as God's creations, and preserve and use to the glory of God those which He has placed in your possession.

• Be content with what you have, whether little or much, and give thanks to God for it.

• Form no attachment of the passions for anything.

• Regard all things as external means and instruments, so as to be free in your dealings with them; do not allow them to become restraints and obstacles in your righteous endeavors. Do not allow yourself to lean on these fragile supports.

• Do not boast of your possessions. Do not envy the possessions of someone else.

• Avoid acquisitiveness. Do not be extravagant in things which are not good.

Actually, everyone is obligated to observe all these things every day of his or her life, in one form or another—almost at every step. Thus, if we "live honorably," we will have a "good conscience," imitating Saint Paul (Hebrews 13:18).

People "desiring to live honorably" and eager for salvation behave as we have set forth above, trying not to go wrong in any of these things and not to stain their consciences. Still, in spite of their efforts, things slip through—wrong thoughts and feelings, wrong words, or wrong behavior.

Sometimes these are unnoticed; sometimes we are aware of them. In either case they cover the pure face of conscience with dust, so that toward the end of the day hardly any of us escapes looking like a hiker who has walked along a dusty trail—dust clinging to our eyes, nose, mouth, and hair, covering our whole face.

That is why all of us, if we are eager and earnest for salvation, have the task of examining our conscience in the evening. Then, taking note of all the wrong things which gained admittance to our thoughts, words, and actions, we must wash them off with repentance—do, in other words, what the dusty hiker does. The hiker washes with water, but we cleanse ourselves with repentance, contrition, and tears.

This self-examination must put everything to the test—

both good and bad, right and wrong—from all the sides we have set forth above. If we see something right in itself, we must still examine it to see:

• whether it was right in impulse and intention;

• whether it was right in the manner used to put it into practice;

• whether it was right in the attitude we had toward it after it was completed, that is, whether it was done for effect, for gaining favor with other people, or for self-indulgence;

• whether it was fitting, timely, and in the right place;

• whether, having done it, we blew our own trumpet and praised ourselves, instead of giving praise to God.

A good deed is truly good when it is done through obedience to God's will and to the glory of God, with absolute renunciation and forgetfulness of self.

If we find something wrong in ourselves, let us examine how we happened to do this even though we have a constant desire to do only what is right. Proceeding in that manner, we must next seek to determine both the external and internal causes; how we should have controlled ourselves on this occasion, so as not to sin; why we did not so control ourselves.

Then, without blaming things or people, but blaming only ourselves, the next step is to sensibly determine how to behave in the future to avoid sinning in these or similar circumstances. We can then establish a firm rule to carry out our decision without exception, self-indulgence, or seeking favors—thus using even impurities to fertilize the field of our heart.

When the examination is finished, we must give thanks to God for everything that was right—without crediting any part to ourselves, for as we very well know, "it is God who works in you both to will and to do for His good pleasure" (Philippians 2:13). And without Him, we cannot do anything good (John 15:5).

So we render thanks to God, and imitating Saint Paul, forget what is past, and increase our zeal, "reaching forward to those things which are ahead" (Philippians 3:13). As to the wrong things, we must repent and be contrite before the Lord, blaming ourselves for the fact that the loaves we bring Him as our offering are never quite pure, for they are always mixed with chaff and impurities. Then we must make a firm resolution to watch ourselves closely the following day, not allowing anything wrong to slip through—not only in words and deeds, but in thoughts and feelings as well.

Those who watch themselves will do all this—the examination and the actions that result from it—during the very course of the day, so that in the evening their examination of their conscience becomes only a repetition of what has already been made during the day—its correction and amplification.

This is, after all, the better method, and more natural at that. For consider: no wrong we have done can be hidden from the conscience. And having once noticed it, the conscience immediately becomes troubled. Certainly, then, it is more natural to calm it at once by self-condemnation, contrition, and the decision to behave correctly in the future, than to leave it all until evening!

There are, however, a few more things to be said on the subject:

• We must strictly examine our actions, exploring why we do what we do, rendering a merciless verdict upon ourselves for our wrongdoing. The more deeply we explore all that happens within us and comes from us, eliminating all wrong things and affirming right things, the more quickly we will be able to cleanse our conscience—just as the deeper the well, the purer the water.

• Once our conscience has learned what is right and what is wrong, it will always demand right behavior—and pursue with condemnation and remorse any tolerance of wrong behavior. But until it reaches full knowledge of what is right and what is wrong, or until it has its "senses exercised to discern both good and evil" (Hebrews 5:14), so that it possesses within itself eyes to see, it will remain in this sense dependent to some extent on the other powers of the soul—and especially on the judgment of reason.

There is still a problem there, however, for until the heart is purified of sinful passions, reason is often bribed by them and produces justifications of our actions—justifications which cloud the eye of conscience and mislead it into accepting black for white. Therefore, as long as we are still struggling with passions, we must examine ourselves by placing our deeds before the mirror of the Word of God and be guided by what we see there in determining their quality and value. Furthermore, we must not be lazy or hesitant about paying frequent visits to our spiritual father or guide.

• We must begin and end the examination of our deeds and behavior with diligent prayer, asking the Lord to give us eyes to see the innermost depths of our heart, for "the heart is deceitful above all things, and desperately wicked; who can know it?" (Jeremiah 17:9). The answer is: No one but God, who is "greater than our heart, and knows all things" (1 John 3:20). "For You, only You, know the hearts of all the children of men" (1 Kings 8:39). There are wrong feelings hidden deeply in our hearts. At times they slip out into our actions; at times they are not even noticed, but they pollute those actions with the stench of sin. Thus, we must pray with David the Prophet: "Cleanse me from secret faults" (Psalm 19:12).

STUDY QUESTIONS

WARMING A COLD, DRY HEART
1. *How would you define spiritual warmth of heart?*
2. *How should we go about building spiritual warmth of heart?*
3. *What can we do to help preserve spiritual warmth of heart once we have experienced it?*

ENDURING COOLNESS WITH PATIENCE
1. *How can we determine whether coolness of heart is our own fault, or is sent by God?*
2. *If coolness is sent to us by God, how should we respond to this? Where can we turn for encouragement?*

GUARDING OUR CONSCIENCE
1. *Which of the four relationships mentioned is most important for you to work on right now? Why?*

2. *How does the illustration of the hiker who gets dusty apply to your experience?*
3. *How can you apply the section on self-examination to your life today?*

CHAPTER 7

Establishing and Preserving Peace of Heart

ON SPIRITUAL PEACE OF HEART

Our heart is made by God for the sole purpose of loving Him and of serving as a dwelling place for Him. So He calls to each of us to give Him our heart, saying: "My son, give me your heart, and let your eyes observe my ways" (Proverbs 23:26).

Since God is peace passing all understanding, it is necessary for the heart which wishes to receive Him to be peaceful, free from turmoil. For, as David writes, the place of God is that of peace. We must, therefore, endeavor to firmly establish peace in our heart. All our virtues, all our efforts and endeavors should be directed toward acquiring this peace—especially our courageous acts of struggle against the enemies of our salvation. One writer has said, "Make your major concern the conforming of yourself to God inside. Then you will conquer your outer passions."

Peace of heart is disturbed by sinful passions. So if we do not allow those passions to approach our heart, it will always remain at peace. In the unseen warfare, the warrior (that is us) must stand fully armed, as it were, at the gates of the heart and drive back all those who attempt to enter and disturb it. When our heart is at peace, victory over attackers is not difficult.

Peace of heart is both the aim of spiritual warfare and the most powerful means to attain victory in it. So when the turmoil of passions finds its way into our heart, we must not jump to attack the passion in order to overcome it. Rather, we must quickly descend into our heart and devote ourselves to restoring quiet there. As soon as our heart becomes quiet, the struggle is over.

Human life is literally made up of unceasing warfare and endless temptation. Temptation causes struggle and so warfare results. Because of this warfare, let us always keep awake, doing our utmost to guard our heart, to watch over it, and keep it peaceful and quiet. When some disturbing activity arises in our soul, let us labor to squelch it and pacify our heart—lest this confusion cause us to stray from the right path.

It is said that the human heart can be compared to the weight on an old-fashioned pendulum wall clock or to the rudder of a boat. If the weight is made lighter or heavier, the movement of the wheels of the clock will change and the hands will no longer show the correct time. And if we move a boat's rudder to the left or to the right, the course of the boat is altered, so that it is no longer on its former course.

In the same way, when our heart is thrown into turmoil, everything within us is thrown out of kilter and our spirit itself loses the capacity to think properly. This is why it is necessary for us not to delay in quieting our heart as soon as it becomes troubled by something internal or external—whether when we are in prayer or at some other time.

We must also realize that we will not learn how to pray until we have truly mastered the task of guarding our inner peace. We must therefore give attention to this task and try to find out how to achieve a state of being in which everything we do is done in peace of heart—with pleasure and joy.

Note therefore: Preserving peace of heart should be a constant activity of our life. We must never allow our heart to be thrown into disorderly turmoil. Then, doing all our business tranquilly, in the shelter of this peace (as it is written, "My son, go on with your business in meekness [tranquillity]" Ecclesiasticus 3:17), we will attain the blessedness promised to the tranquil: "Blessed are the meek, for they shall inherit the earth" (Matthew 5:5).

PRESERVING INNER PEACE

Here is some practical help toward achieving inner peace.

First of all, we must keep our five outer senses in order and keep our external conduct calm, collected, and under control. When we become accustomed to calm and collected behavior in our external movements and actions, we will find it easier to acquire inner peace in our heart. For according to the testimony of the Fathers, our inner life takes its cue from our outer life.

Second, we must establish in ourselves an intention to love all people and to live in harmony with everyone—as Saint Paul teaches: "If it is possible, as much as depends on you, live peaceably with all men" (Romans 12:18).

Third, we must keep our conscience clean, so that it

does not gnaw at us or reproach us in anything, but is at peace in relation to God, to ourselves, to our neighbors, and to all external things. If we keep our conscience clean, it will produce, deepen, and strengthen inner peace. As David says: "Great peace have those who love Your law, and nothing causes them to stumble" (Psalm 119:165).

Fourth, we must accustom ourselves to bear unpleasantness and insults without becoming upset or agitated. Until we have acquired this habit, we will have to grieve and suffer a great deal in our heart through lack of experience in controlling ourselves in situations of this kind. Once we have acquired this habit, however, our soul will find great comfort in the very troubles we encounter. If we are determined, we will learn day by day to manage ourselves better and better. And we will, in the process, reach a state of spirit and heart in which we will know how to preserve the peace of our spirit in all storms, both inner and outer.

If we find there are times when we are unable to manage our heart and restore peace in it by driving away all stress and grief, the answer is to go to prayer. We must be persistent about it, imitating our Lord and Savior, who prayed three times in the garden of Gethsemane—to show us by His example that prayer should be our refuge in every time of stress and distress of our heart.

And, in fact, His example demonstrates that no matter how fainthearted and anguished we may be, we are not to abandon prayer until we reach a state in which our will is in complete accord with the will of God. That will be a state of being in which, calmed by this agreement, our heart is filled with courageous daring, joyfully ready to meet, accept, and bear the very thing it feared and wished to avoid. In just this way our Lord felt fear, sorrow, and grief, but, regaining peace through prayer, said calmly: "Rise, let us be going. See, my betrayer is at hand" (Matthew 26:46).

PEACE OF HEART COMES GRADUALLY

We must watch constantly to keep our heart from becoming agitated or distressed, using every effort to keep it peaceful and calm. Seeing our efforts and endeavors, God will send us His grace and will make our soul a city of peace. Then our heart will become a house of comfort like that mentioned allegorically in the psalm: "Jerusalem is built as a city" (Psalm 122:3). God requires only one thing: that when we are disturbed by something, we immediately restore peace within ourselves—thus remaining undisturbed in all our activities and duties.

All this requires patience—for just as a city is not built in a day, we cannot expect to gain inner peace in a day. Achieving inner peace means building a house for the God of peace, a tabernacle for the Almighty—in this way becoming a temple of God. Remember, it is God Himself who builds this house within us, and without Him all our labor will be in vain, as is written: "Unless the LORD builds the house, they labor in vain who build it" (Psalm 127:1).

We must also be aware that the main foundations of this peace of heart are humility and the avoidance of activities, works, and occupations which bring worry and anxiety.

As to the first, we all know that humility, peace of heart, and meekness are so closely related that where one is present, the others are as well. If our heart is at peace and we are meek, we are also humble. And if we are humble in heart, we are also meek and at peace. That is why our Lord joined these qualities inseparably together, saying: "Take My yoke upon you and learn from Me, for I am gentle [meek] and lowly in heart, and you will find rest for your souls" (Matthew 11:29).

As regards the second foundation (avoidance of activities, works, and occupations which bring worry and anxiety), we see the prototype of its application in the Old Testament. God indicated He wished His house to be built not by David, who spent almost all his life in wars and tribulations, but by his son Solomon, who, living by his name (Solomon means peaceable), was a peaceful king who fought no one.

AVOID HONORS, LOVE HUMILITY

As we noted previously, if we love peace of heart, we must labor to enter it by the door of humility—simply because there is no other door. And, in order to acquire humility, we must force ourselves to welcome with a loving embrace and as beloved sisters all hardships and tribulations. We must also flee all fame and honors, preferring to be unknown and scorned by everyone—receiving no care or consolation from anyone but God.

Our task is to establish firmly in our heart the view that God is our only good, our sole refuge—and everything else is no better than thorns which will cause us mortal harm if we take them into our heart. If we happen to be put to shame by someone, we are not to mourn over it, but rather to bear it with joy—convinced that God is with us.

Nor should we seek any honor or have any desire other than to suffer for the love we have for God and for those things that magnify His glory.

Let us also exhort and require ourselves to rejoice when we are insulted, condemned, or scorned. Ill-treatment and disgrace such as this conceal a great treasure, and if we willingly accept it, we will become rich in spirit—all unknown to those who have done us a service by bringing this disgrace upon us. Nor should we seek love or honor in this life—for without them we will be more free to suffer with the crucified Christ, meeting no hindrance to this from anyone or anything.

We must watch out for our own self as our worst enemy, not following our own will, mind, taste, or feeling—if we wish to avoid getting lost. Thus, we must always be fully armed against ourselves. When our desire inclines toward something—however holy—we must strip our desire of anything extraneous and place it, alone, before God with the greatest humility, imploring Him that in this matter His will and not our own may be done. This we must do with a sincere and heartfelt surrender of ourselves to the will of God—with no trace of self-love (insofar as we can tell)—knowing we have nothing in ourselves and can do nothing by ourselves to work our salvation.

We must guard ourselves from thoughts which appear holy and arouse an unreasonable zeal for themselves. The Lord speaks in the Gospel in words that may be understood allegorically to refer to these thoughts: "Beware of false prophets, who come to you in sheep's clothing, but inwardly they are ravenous wolves. You will know them by their fruit" (Matthew 7:15, 16). The fruit of these thoughts is the decline and breaking of the spirit.

All those things which draw us away from humility— and from inner peace and quiet—however beautiful they may seem, must be seen as "false prophets." Hiding under the cover of sheep's clothing (that is, of a hypocritical zeal to do good to our neighbors without discernment), they are actually marauding wolves, who will rob us of the humility, peace, and quiet so necessary to everyone who desires steady progress in spiritual life.

The more the external appearance of an action seems holy, the more carefully we must examine it—though without excitement or agitation. If we sometimes happen to fall into error in this process, let us not be dejected, but simply humble ourselves before God, and, conscious of our weakness, use it as a lesson for the future. After all, it may just be that God has allowed it to happen in order to break some concealed feature of pride which we do not suspect.

If we feel our soul pierced by a barb of the poisonous thorn (that is, by sinful passion or a thought provoked by passion), we must not become agitated, but increase our attention and endeavor to keep that thorn from reaching our heart. The thing to do is to meet such attacks face to face, resisting them, keeping our heart behind us, out of reach and pure before God.

Thus, because our heart remains pure, we will always have God present in the depths of our heart. At the same time, we must fill our inner being with the conviction that everything that happens to us and in us is a test and an education—designed to teach us in the end to truly perceive things which lead to our salvation. Following these things we can be made worthy to receive the crown of truth, prepared for us by God's lovingkindness.

DETACHED, CALM, AND PEACEFUL SOULS

The God of gods and Lord of lords (compare Deuteronomy 10:17; Joshua 22:22) created our soul to be a dwelling place, a temple for Himself. Let us, therefore, hold our soul in great respect, keeping it from becoming corrupted by inclining toward something lower than itself—meanwhile keeping our desires and hopes centered on this invisible presence of God with us. God visits the soul He finds calm and peaceful, free, insofar as possible, of all other thoughts and desires—and above all, free of a contrary will of its own.

In connection with this latter, we must not undertake any strict endeavors or voluntary self-denial of our own accord and without proper deliberation. Nor should we seek opportunities to suffer for the love of God, obeying only the suggestions of our own will. For such activities we must have the advice of our spiritual father, who guides us as God's representative. Our task is to obey him in all things, and through him God will direct our will toward what He Himself wills—that which is most useful for us.

Never should we do anything just because we want to, that is, by our own will alone. We should always let God Himself do in us just what He wants from us. It is best, in fact, to learn to have no wishes of our own—and even if we do, to be so set on God's will that whether what we wanted happens or not, we will not be at all upset, but remain serene in spirit, as if we had not wished for anything.

Such an attitude and disposition is true freedom, detachment, and tranquillity of the heart—for then we are not tied down either by our heart or by our will in relation to anything. If we present our soul to God thus emptied, free, and undivided, we will finally witness the miraculous works He will perform in it. Above all, however, He will surround us with divine peace—a gift which will become within us a container for all other gifts, as Gregory Palamas says (in his "Word to the Nun Xenia," Greek Philokalia, page 944):

> O wonderful union, secret treasure-house of the Almighty, the only place He consents to listen to the words you address to Him, and Himself speaks with the heart of your soul! O desert and solitude which has become a paradise! For there alone God allows us to see Him and talk with Him. 'I will now turn aside and see this great sight, why the bush does not burn' (Exodus 3:3), says Moses in the desert of Sinai, a physical place, yet rich in inner contemplations. If you wish to be worthy of the same, step in this place unshod, for this ground is holy. First bare your feet, that is, the disposition of your soul, and let them be stripped and free of every earthly thing. Carry neither purse nor scrip traveling this way, as the Lord commanded His

disciples (Luke 10:4). You should no longer desire anything from this world and should greet no one along the way, as Elisha instructed his servant and the Lord commanded His disciples. Your whole thought, whole disposition, and whole love should be turned only to God and not to any creatures—'Let the dead bury their own dead' (Matthew 8:22). Walk alone in the land of the living, and may death have no part in you.

STUDY QUESTIONS

ON SPIRITUAL PEACE OF HEART

1. *How would you keep your heart peaceful in the midst of an unhappy work situation? In the midst of assisting a child through a difficult school situation? In the midst of sorting out financial problems?*

PRESERVING INNER PEACE

1. *Which do you see to be the most important of the four points given at the beginning of the section? Why?*
2. *Which of the points at the beginning of the section strikes closest to your own heart—as being the area in which you need to do the most work?*

PEACE OF HEART COMES GRADUALLY

1. *Consider the two elements which make up the foundation of peace of heart. How do they promote this peace?*
2. *Describe how the discussion in this section relates to your own experience—and how it may help you.*

AVOID HONORS, LOVE HUMILITY

1. *How can we judge the appropriateness of an action that seems holy?* /how you feel ahead

2. *What has been your experience with struggling against yourself? What specific help for that struggle do you find in the information and advice in this section?* I don't take myself too seriously.

DETACHED, CALM, AND PEACEFUL SOULS

1. *What is the benefit to be derived from keeping our soul hidden from and unmoved by the things going on around us?* I like to keep secret between God and myself. It makes me feel good inside and smile outside.

CHAPTER 8

Putting God First in our Lives

WORKS OF LOVE TOWARD NEIGHBORS

There can be no limit placed on love for God, just as our beloved God Himself has no bounds or limits. But love for our neighbor must have bounds and limits. If we do not keep it within the right limits, it may turn us away from the love of God, cause us great harm, and lead us to destruction.

We certainly must love our neighbor, but our love must not be allowed to cause harm to our soul. We must therefore do all our works in a manner both simple and holy, with nothing in view but to please God. This will protect us from making any false steps out of love for our neighbor.

The most important work we can do on behalf of our neighbors is to assist in their salvation. But our own ill-considered and rash zeal can interfere in these actions, bringing nothing but harm to both our neighbors and ourselves. What we want is to be an example of sincere faith and of a life pleasing to God—then, like the Apostles, we will be the fragrance of Christ (see 2 Corinthians 2:25), drawing all people to follow Him.

But we must not urge everyone indiscriminately with our words, calling upon them to come to Him. If we do that, we will destroy not only our peace with others, but our own inner peace as well. It is proper to have a fervent zeal and strong desire for everyone to know the truth in the same degree of perfection we know it—and to be intoxicated with this wine, which God has promised and which He now gives without price (Isaiah 55:1). We must, in fact, always have this thirst for the salvation of our neighbors. But it must rise out of our love of God and not from indiscreet or rash eagerness.

God Himself will plant such love for our brothers and sisters in our soul when it has renounced all things, and will come in His own time to gather its fruit. But we must not sow anything of our own accord. All we have to do is to offer God the soil of our heart, free of all weeds and thistles, and He will sow the seed in it—when and how He wills. This seed will bear fruit in its proper time.

We must remember: God wishes to see our soul withdrawn from everything else in order to unite it with Himself. Thus, we can leave it to Him to act in us—and we must not hinder His work by interference on the part of our will. Make no plans for yourself but one—always seek to please God by obeying His will.

The Gospel parable tells us the farmer has already gone out to find laborers for his vineyard. Keeping that in mind, we must put away all worry and all thought, strip ourselves of all anxiety about ourselves and all attachment of the passions to anything material, of this world, and God will clothe us in Himself and give us things we cannot even imagine. Wholly forget about yourself, as much as you can, and let only the love of God live in your soul.

Furthermore, if we learn to use prudence and restrain our zeal in relation to others, the Lord will preserve us in peace and serenity of soul. In the meantime, we must watch carefully to keep our soul from suffering loss in its primary blessing—peace of heart—because of foolish worries about the blessings of others. The source of this blessing is total obedience of our soul to God—together with renunciation of all things.

This we are to do, but not expecting reward, and never allowing the thought that we can do something worthy of reward. God Himself acts in all things and expects nothing from us but humility before Him, and the gift of our soul—freed from all earthly things—with only one wish in the depths of our heart: to have God's will fulfilled in us, always and in all things.

THE SURRENDERED SOUL

Our calling as Christians is to trust in God, who calls all people, saying, "Come to Me, all you who labor and are heavy laden, and I will give you rest" (Matthew 11:28), and to follow this call, trusting at the same time in the coming of the Holy Spirit.

We must, in effect, plunge with eyes closed into the sea of divine Providence and compassion, not resisting with our own will, letting the mighty waves of God's will carry us, like some inanimate thing, to the harbor of salvation and Christian perfection.

It is good to practice this resting many times a day, seeking inner and outer solitude as much as possible so as to consecrate all the powers of our soul to those practices which are effective in producing in us a strong love of God. These practices include prayer, unceasing calling upon the name of our Lord and Savior Jesus Christ, tears flowing from love for Him, warm and joy-giving adoration of Him, and other spiritual works.

We must allow these works to be performed in us freely, without forcing and coercing our heart—lest we foolishly exhaust ourselves by compulsory activities, thus becoming hardened and incapable of receiving the influence of grace. We must find and take the advice of experienced Christians, using that advice to guide our attempt to acquire the habit of constant contemplation of God's holiness and His countless blessings. And we must accept those blessings with humility.

But let us not constantly besiege God with requests for such displays of His goodness. It is better to remain humbly in our inner seclusion, in our heart, waiting for God's will to be done in us. And when God grants our requests without excessive effort on our part, we will experience joy and fruitfulness. The key which opens the treasure-house of spiritual gifts of knowledge and divine love is composed of humility, self-renunciation, and surrender to God at all times and in everything. The same key locks the door to ignorance and spiritual coldness.

Let us love as much as we can to sit with Mary at the feet of Christ our Lord and listen to what He has to say to our soul. We must beware lest our enemies (the greatest of whom is ourselves) frustrate this holy standing in silence before the Lord. When we seek God with our spirit, to come to rest in Him, it is wrong to assign Him any place or boundaries by our narrow and impotent fantasy. He has no limit and is everywhere and in everything—or rather, all things are in Him. We will find Him in ourselves, in our soul, every time we truly seek Him. God Himself desires to be with us, the children of Adam, to make us worthy of Him—although He has no need of us.

When we read the Holy Scriptures, the proper method is not to have it in our minds to read, page after page, but rather to reflect over each word. When some words make us go deeply into ourselves or stir us to repentance, or fill our heart with spiritual joy and love, let us pause with them. The stirring they give us means that God draws near us, so that we may receive Him humbly with an open heart— for He Himself wishes us to partake of Him.

If the pause causes us to fail to complete the reading we have planned, that is nothing to worry about. We simply need to remember that the purpose of all spiritual exercises is to help us become worthy to partake of the Lord. And when that partaking is granted, there is no point in worrying about means. In the same way, when we reflect on some divine subject, especially some aspect of the suffering of Christ our Lord, let us pause at any part that touches our heart, keeping our attention on it longer to prolong this touch of God.

One of the great obstacles to preserving inner peace is binding ourselves by some unchangeable law—a set and undeviating rule—to read, say, so many psalms, so many chapters from the Gospels, and so many chapters from the Epistles. After we have set such rules for ourselves, we sometimes get in a hurry to complete the readings, forgetting to concern ourselves with whether our heart is touched by them or not—or whether spiritual thoughts and contemplations arise in our mind. Then, if we fail to finish the reading, we become agitated and worried—not because we were deprived of the spiritual fruit of reading (which we need in order to create a new man in ourselves), but simply because we didn't get everything read.

On this subject, Saint Isaac the Syrian writes:

> If you wish to obtain joy from reading texts and understand the words of the Spirit, brush aside the quantity and number of verses, so that your mind can be absorbed in studying the words of the Spirit, until, filled with wonder at the divine dispensation, your soul is aroused to a lofty understanding of them and is thus moved to praise of God or to sorrow that benefits the soul. Slavish work brings no peace to the mind. And anxiety usually deprives the reason and understanding of the power of taste, and robs the thoughts like a leech, which sucks life from the body along with the blood of its members.

If we sincerely desire to complete the course of our present life virtuously, we must have no other aim than to find God wherever He chooses to show Himself to us. When this is given to us, we must stop all other activity—and not go back to it. Forget everything else and rest only in God.

When the Almighty chooses to withdraw from us and ceases manifesting His nearness to us in some given instant, then we can turn once more to our usual spiritual activities. Then we can continue with those activities, having the same aim in view—to find our Beloved through them, and, having found Him, to stop once more and rest in Him alone. All this is very important. There are many people engaged in spiritual work who deprive themselves of the saving fruits of peace derived from their spiritual works, because they persist in those works, afraid to suffer loss if they do not complete them, convinced (wrongly, of course) that this constitutes spiritual perfection.

So it goes. Following their own will (which they do not really desire to do), they drive and torment themselves greatly—but still receive no real quiet, nor the inner peace in which God truly dwells and has His rest.

BEWARE OF PLEASURES AND COMFORTS

For the good of your soul: Always choose what is difficult and painful, and do not love pleasures and comforts, which do not profit your soul.

We must learn to love being in a subordinate position, dependent upon the will of others. Every action we take should be a step bringing us nearer to God—we should let no action we take become an obstacle on this path. This must be our joy. God alone should be the delight of our heart, and everything else bitterness in comparison.

Let us, then, offer to God every hardship we encounter. We are called to love Him and surrender all our heart to Him, without deliberation or fear. And He will show the means to solve all our dilemmas and raise us up if we fall. In a word: if we love God, we will receive every blessing from Him. Thus, let us offer the whole of ourselves as a sacrifice to God, in peace and quiet of spirit.

In order to make progress on this path—and free it from weariness and confusion—we must first place our will in God's will. The more completely we succeed in placing it there, keeping nothing for ourselves, the more strength and comfort we will achieve. The point is to let our will be so attuned that we desire only what God wishes—and desire nothing He does not. Continually, and with every action, we must renew the intention and desire of our soul to please God in all things. Nor should we make plans for the future, since we "do not know what a day may bring forth" (Proverbs 27:1).[7]

In everything we undertake, let us keep a firm resolve to do all we can, all that is needed, and all that is obligatory for us—but to be indifferent to everything else and submit humbly to whatever outer results may follow.

The thing we can always do is sacrifice our will to God. There is nothing better or more to wish for. If we keep to that, we will always enjoy freedom and, bound by nothing from any side, will always rejoice and be at peace with ourselves. This freedom of spirit constitutes the great blessing we read about in the writings of the saints. It is nothing more (nor less) than a steady abiding in our inner self—with no desire emerging from our inner fortress to seek something outside.

As long as we keep ourselves free in this manner, we will continue to partake of that divine and inexpressible joy which is inseparable from the kingdom of God, established within us, as the Lord says: "The kingdom of God is within you" (Luke 17:21).

STUDY QUESTIONS

WORKS OF LOVE TOWARD NEIGHBORS
1. *Have you ever had the experience of helping someone and then realizing that your help probably hindered rather than benefitted their spiritual development? How did it all come about? What would you do if faced with the situation again?*
2. *What about your own spiritual condition—has your attempt to help someone else interfered with the peace of your heart? How?*

THE SURRENDERED SOUL
1. *What has been your experience of surrender to God?*
2. *Discuss the words of Saint Isaac the Syrian given in this section.*
3. *Have you ever pushed yourself to complete some spiritual activity, such as reading the Scriptures, and in the process come to some passage which attracted you to God in an unusual way? How did you handle it?*

BEWARE OF PLEASURES AND COMFORTS
1. *How does the first sentence of this section strike you?*
2. *How can you fulfill the admonitions in this section in your own life, without abdicating any of your responsibilities?*

CHAPTER 9

If Inner Peace Withdraws

WHEN PEACE IS INTERRUPTED

Those who follow the path of God often experience times when the holy peace, that glorious inner seclusion of calm detachment, and the freedom they love are interrupted—when, in fact, they withdraw. Sometimes movements within the heart raise such clouds of dust within that one cannot see the path one must follow.

When we happen to experience something like this, we must realize and recognize that God allows it to happen for our own good. This is precisely the warfare for which God has rewarded His saints with radiant crowns. Remembering this, then, let us not lose courage in the trials we face. As in any other trouble, we may look to the Lord and say to Him from our heart, "O Lord my God, take care of Your servant, and let Your will be done in me. I know and confess that Your words and promises are true. I put my trust in them and stand firmly upon Your path." Blessed is the soul that surrenders to the Lord each time it experiences trouble and hardship.

If, in spite of this, the struggle persists and we are unable to attune and unite our will with the will of God as quickly as we wish, let us not mourn or lose heart, but continue to surrender ourselves to God, bowing willingly to His decisions. Through this we will gain victory. Remember the battle our Lord Jesus Christ had to fight in the garden of Gethsemane, when He cried, "O My Father, if it is possible, let this cup pass from Me." But He immediately added, "Nevertheless, not as I will, but as You will" (Matthew 26:39). For He indeed faced all we have to face.

When we are faced with difficulties, it is best not to take any step till we raise our eyes to the crucified Christ our Lord. There we will see written in large letters how we too should behave in the hardships which face us. So let us copy it for ourselves—not in letters and words, but in actions. That is, when we feel attacks of self-loving self-pity, we must not pay attention to them nor crawl down from our cross. Let us rather resort to prayer and endure with humility—striving to conquer our will and to stand firmly in the determination to desire God's will to be done in us.

If we emerge from our prayer with this fruit, let us rejoice. If we fail to attain it, our soul will be left fasting, not having tasted its natural fruit.

We must try to let nothing dwell in our soul except God—even for a short time. In the meantime, do not mourn or be distressed by anything. Nor should we turn our eyes to look at the evil of others or to bad examples. Rather, let us learn to be like a little child, which, in its innocence, does not notice such things, but passes them by unharmed.

THE WILES OF THE ENEMY AND INNER PEACE

Our enemy, the devil, rejoices when our soul is confused and our heart is agitated. When this happens, he applies his shrewd skills in trying to upset our souls.

The first of his means is to arouse self-love, hoping he can cause withdrawal of that grace which creates and preserves inner peace. With this goal, he suggests to us the idea that all the things which are (and which appear) good in us have been acquired by our own hard work and diligence. Dismissing humility and simplicity, he tries to cause us to put a high value on and ascribe great consequence to ourselves—to feel we are something very important. He works to cause us to veil in forgetfulness the action of divine grace—that grace without which no one can even say the Lord's name, as Saint Paul testifies: "No one can say that Jesus is Lord except by the Holy Spirit" (1 Corinthians 12:3).

Now this grace, which is so crucial to us, is given to all believers, and its presence is a sign that one is a true believer. Having received it, a believer no longer does—nor can do—anything truly good without its help. It remains with us always, according to the Lord's promise. And the enemy can do nothing with us while that grace is in us and surrounds us. That is why the devil tries every means imaginable to make it withdraw—and the first thing he does, as we noted above, is to suggest self-appreciation, or feelings that we are not insignificant, but truly something important.

If we accept such suggestions, the enemy offers a new idea: that we are certainly better than other people, more zealous and richer in good works. Once he succeeds in getting us to adopt this opinion, the devil is in a position to expand it—which he does, leading us to judge and despise others, a practice which is invariably followed by pride. All this can take place in our heart in the course of a single moment. Even so, the action of grace is immediately reduced, resulting in lack of attention to ourselves, weakening of zeal, and the rising up of empty thoughts. Empty thoughts then lead to thoughts which are directed by the passions, followed by stirrings of the sinful passions themselves.

This change is inseparably linked with a storm which rages in our heart—inner peace is lost. This state of affairs is not permanent, and if we remember ourselves, we are filled with contrition, repent, and by prayer reestablish our customary inner order. The enemy is banished, but he does not lose heart, returning again and again with the same suggestions for the same purpose—to destroy our inner peace.

Knowing this—and in order to oppose these hostile efforts of our enemy—we must watch ourselves carefully, remembering the words of our Lord: "Watch and pray, lest you enter into temptation. The spirit indeed is willing, but the flesh is weak" (Matthew 26:41). Thus, our watch over ourselves must be truly diligent, lest our enemy creep up and rob us, depriving us of this great treasure: inner peace and quiet of soul.

The devil strives to destroy the peace of our soul because he knows that when our soul is in turmoil it is more easily led into sin. Guarding our peace is essential, for we know that when our soul is peaceful, the enemy cannot get to it. It is also ready for all good things and does them willingly and without difficulty, easily overcoming all obstacles.

To succeed more easily in this, it is best to try to anticipate the moves of the enemy. His most likely move is to attempt to implant a self-reliant thought in us. The most effective defense is to make it a rule to regard as coming from the enemy every thought which tends to decrease our conviction that all good comes from God—that we cannot succeed in anything without the help of His grace. The conclusion is obvious: we can succeed in nothing without the help of His grace. Therefore we must put all our trust in God alone.

We must regard all thoughts to the contrary as clearly coming from the enemy—and furiously reject them and chase them away till they disappear. The action of the Holy Spirit in us at all times is to lead our souls toward union with God—to kindle in our souls a devout and joyful love of Him, a blessed confidence and steadfast trust in Him. Whatever is opposed to this is the work of the enemy.

We can be sure the devil uses every means and method he can invent to disturb our soul. He introduces into our heart excessive and needless fears, intending to increase the weakness of our soul, preventing it from maintaining the necessary order and from delighting as it should in confession, in Holy Communion, or in prayer. Instead, he attempts to make our soul go through all these fearfully and in confusion rather than with humble boldness and love.

If he can, he makes our soul receive with hopeless sorrow and pain that impoverishment of religious feeling and absence of inner delight which often come in times of prayer or during other spiritual activities. This he does by suggesting to our soul that this impoverishment means that all its efforts and endeavors lead nowhere and are best abandoned. The truth, of course, is that this impoverishment is often allowed by God for the good of our soul.

In this way our enemy (if he can) finally brings our soul to a hopelessness and confusion so great that it actually begins to think that everything it does is indeed useless and fruitless—and that God has completely forgotten and abandoned it.

But the fact is, you see, this is clearly a lie. A soul may experience dryness and an impoverishment of religious feeling and spiritual joy. Nevertheless, in spite of this, it can perform all kinds of good actions, moved by simple faith and armed with holy patience and consistency. Still, we may better understand it (and escape suffering harm when God finds it desirable to send or to allow dryness and impoverishment for our own good), if we take a look at the blessings which come from humble patience in times of dryness and coldness of heart.

We will deal with this next—so we can learn not to lose our peace of soul and not to be eaten up by sorrow when we have to suffer either this or some other disturbing thoughts and impulses of passions.

WHEN WE LACK SPIRITUAL FEELINGS

We are all plagued at times by dryness and cooling of the heart—and by the sadness these bring to our soul. There is, however, some advantage to these unpleasant conditions: namely, this grief and dryness of heart or lack of spiritual joy and sweetness bring much benefit to our soul if we accept and endure them with humility and patience.

If we knew of this benefit beforehand, we would surely not consider this condition a burden—nor be grieved when we have to face it. For then we would not be thinking of this unhappy lack of inner spiritual comforts as a sign of God's displeasure; we would be able to accept it as the work of God's particular love for us. We would, in fact, gladly accept it as a great mercy.

In fact, we may, from the very start, be comforted by the very fact that these spiritual conditions are usually experienced by people who give themselves up with the greatest of zeal to the service of God—and give special attention to avoiding anything that may offend Him. And these godly people experience these conditions not when they are first converted, but when they have worked for God for a considerable time—when their heart has been sufficiently purified by prayer and contrition; when they have felt a certain spiritual sweetness, warmth, and joy which made them consecrate themselves completely to God; and when they have already begun to do so in practice.

Nor do we find that sinners, or people addicted to the various frivolities and conceits of the world and of daily life, ever have such experiences or are subjected to such temptations. This should demonstrate clearly that such bitter experience is an honorable and precious banquet— to which the Lord invites those He loves best.

And though its taste is not pleasant when we eat it, we are benefited greatly by it, even if we don't see this at the time. For when our soul is in this state of dryness, when it tastes this bitterness and suffers temptations and thoughts the mere memory of which make us tremble, it poisons the heart and almost kills the inner man. But when the soul finds itself in this condition, it learns to distrust itself and not to rely on its own good state (when it is experiencing it), and so acquires true humility—which God wants so very much for us to have.

Furthermore, the soul then becomes motivated with a desire to acquire a fervent love for God, a diligent attention to its thoughts, and great courage to endure such temptations without harm. The soul comes out of this struggle with "senses exercised to discern both good and evil" (Hebrews 5:14). But since these good fruits are hidden from the sight of the soul, I repeat once more: it is troubled and flees from the bitterness of the experience, for it does not wish to be deprived of its spiritual comforts for even a short time. Consequently, it regards every spiritual activity not accompanied by them as wasted time and useless labor.

EVERY TEMPTATION IS SENT FOR OUR GOOD

It is important for us to understand that all temptations in general are sent or allowed by God for our benefit. Our tendency is to be proud, to love self-glorification and self-display, to hold tight to our own opinions and decisions, and always to want everyone to rate us higher than we deserve.

Self-appreciation and high opinion of ourselves are especially harmful in the work of spiritual endeavor—so much so that even a shadow of them is enough to prevent us from reaching true perfection. Consequently, in His wise provision for us all (and especially for those who have sincerely given themselves over to His service), our loving heavenly Father allows temptations to attack us. This He does to help lead us to a state of being in which we can easily escape this terrible danger of self-appreciation—and are almost forced to come to a truly humble knowledge of ourselves.

He did this with the Apostle Peter by letting him deny Him three times (Matthew 26:34, 69-75)—in order to help him realize his own weakness and learn not to rely on himself. Saint Paul had a similar experience when God, after lifting him to the third heaven and showing him inexpressible divine mysteries (2 Corinthians 12:2), made him endure a certain trying and troublesome temptation so he would bear in himself a mark of his own impotence and insignificance.

This He did so that the greatness of the revelations granted to the Apostle by God would not make him excessively proud—as Saint Paul himself testifies: "And lest I should be exalted above measure by the abundance of the revelations, a thorn in the flesh was given to me, a messenger of Satan to buffet me, lest I be exalted above measure" (2 Corinthians 12:7).

So it is because He is moved by compassion for this unfortunate and lawless tendency we have (to always think highly of ourselves) that God allows all kinds of temptations to plague us—at times very painful ones, so that, remembering our weakness, we will be humbled. In so doing the Lord shows His lovingkindness as well as His wisdom. For by humbling us, He enables us to derive the greatest benefit from things which appear very harmful—

since humility is of all things the most necessary and useful to our soul.

Thus, if all temptations are given to teach us humility, it follows that every servant of God who tastes these bitter states of the heart we have mentioned (dryness, lack of spiritual zest, lack of spiritual comforts in the heart) experiences them in order to learn humility. He comes to think they were brought on by his own sins, that no other soul could be so lacking in all things, that no other soul could work for God as coldly as his soul, that such states only visit those who are abandoned by God, and consequently that he too is abandoned—and deservedly so.

From such humble thoughts a good thing is born: a person who formerly thought of himself as something very important, now, having tasted the bitter medicine sent him from above, begins to consider himself the most sinful man in the world, unworthy even to be called a Christian. And, in very fact, none of us would ever arrive at so humble an opinion of ourselves if we were not moved to do so by those special temptations and, finally, this great sorrow and bitterness of heart.

So such experiences are truly a great mercy which God shows in this life to the soul which surrenders itself to Him, with what we must finally see as wise humility. We must let Him cure us in any way He desires—and, we must add, by the treatments He alone knows perfectly and considers necessary for healing and bringing us to a good condition.

Besides these particular benefits—brought to our soul through these temptations by drastic removal of spiritual comforts—that removal brings many other useful benefits

as well. Made contrite and repentant by these inner bur-
dens, we force ourselves with renewed vigor to run to God
and beg for speedy help from Him; to diligently do everything useful we can think of to cure the sorrow of our soul
and get rid of the distress in our heart; and to avoid this
torment of our soul in the future.

Therefore we make firm resolutions to walk carefully
on the path of spiritual life from now on—paying the
closest possible attention to all movements within our
heart—and to avoid even the slightest shadow of sin and
any little neglect capable of separating us from God and
God from us in any way whatever.

Thus we see that the sorrow we considered so contrary
to our aims (and so harmful), becomes a stimulus motivat-
ing us to seek God with greater warmth—and to avoid
more vigorously everything incompatible with God's will.

In summary, then: All sorrow and suffering the soul
suffers during inner temptations, and the accompanying
scarcity of spiritual comforts and delights, prove to be a
purifying treatment. By their means God, in His
lovingkindness, cleanses the soul if it endures them with
patience and humility. Further, these sufferings ensure, for
those who endure, a crown which can only be gained
through them—a crown made more glorious by more
painful suffering.

So we see from all this that we must not torture ourselves too much or be painfully troubled, either by other
temptations which attack us from without, or by the trials
from within we have been dealing with. We tend to do this,
especially when we have had little experience in these

things. In our lack of familiarity with these things we tend to regard what comes from God as coming from the devil, or from our own sins and imperfections.

In addition we take signs of divine love for signs of divine wrath or judgment, interpreting God's gifts and blessings as punishment brought on us by His displeasure. And we begin to consider all we have done—and are doing—as useless and worthless labors, and our present loss as beyond repair.

But if we accept these inner trials and temptations not as loss of virtue but, on the contrary, as greatly increasing it when we accept them with humility and endure them with thankfulness; if we believe they are arranged by God's loving compassion for us; then we will not be excessively worried and will not lose our peace of heart over the fact that we experience such temptations, have inappropriate and shameful thoughts, and are cold and dry during prayer and other spiritual activities.

All this will then only make our soul more deeply humble before God—and make us resolve in our heart to fulfill God's will in everything we do. For this is what God wants and is pleased to receive from us. We will also resolve to endeavor by every means to keep ourselves peaceful and calm in accepting whatever happens to us as coming from the hand of our heavenly Father—from whom also comes that bitter cup we happen to be drinking at the present moment. For whether a temptation comes from the devil, from other people, or is caused by our sins, it still depends on God and is sent by Him for our good, and to turn some other great temptation away from us.

REMEDY FOR SMALL SINS AND WEAKNESSES

If we have fallen into some small sin of word or deed—if, for example, we are perturbed by some accidental happening; we criticize someone; we listen to such criticism made by others; we enter into argument about something; we are at times impatient, flustered, or suspicious; or if we neglect something—we must not be overly distressed, sad, or despairing in thinking about what we have done.

Above all, we must not aggravate our distress by sad thoughts about ourselves: that it looks as if we will never manage to free ourselves from such weaknesses; that our will to work for the Lord is too weak; or that we are not progressing on the path of the Lord as we should. For every time we do this, we weigh down our soul with thousands of other fears produced by faintness of heart and sadness.

There is good reason for the above warning, for consider what follows if we get overly disturbed: We are ashamed to stand boldly in the presence of God, since we have proved unfaithful to Him. We waste time examining how long we have lingered in every transgression: whether we became identified with it and had begun to desire it or not; whether we had rejected this or that thought or not; and so on.

And the more we torture ourselves in this manner, the more our spirit becomes disorganized and the greater become our stress and our unwillingness to confess our sins. Even if we go to our father confessor, we do so with a disturbing fear, and after confession we still have no peace. It seems to us that we have not said everything.

So we live a bitter, anxious, and fruitless life, wasting much of our time in useless labors. And all this happens because we have forgotten our natural weakness and lost sight of the attitude our soul must have toward God. We have forgotten that when the soul falls into sin, it should turn to God with humble repentance and hope, and not torture itself with excessive sorrow, bitterness, and stress.

For small everyday transgressions, repentance must always be inspired and filled with firm trust in God. And it must be even more so with regard to sins more serious than the ordinary, into which even a zealous servant of God sometimes falls, because God lets it happen. There is good reason for this trust: a penitent distress which tortures the heart and gnaws at it continually can never reestablish hope in the soul if it is not accompanied by a firm trust in the goodness and mercy of God. This trust must always fill the heart of anyone wishing to reach the highest degrees of Christian perfection. Such trust energizes and disciplines all the powers of the soul and the spirit.

Still, many who have entered the path of spiritual life fail to pay attention to this. Consequently, they stop in their progress with their heart weakened and progress no further. They are thus ineligible to receive those blessings of grace which the Lord distributes along this path—and which usually reward only those whose efforts never relax and who move steadfastly on and on.

Above all, however, those who experience some distress in their heart or some confusion, or a split in their conscience, must turn to their spiritual father or someone else experienced in spiritual life. At the same time they must trustfully beg the Lord to reveal the truth through that person (their spiritual father or another such guide) and send them a reassuring solution to their troubles and bewilderment.

Having so done, we must be completely set at rest by the word of our spiritual father or guide.

IF DISTRESSED, CALL OUT!

Every time we fall into a small transgression—even if it happens a thousand times a day—as soon as we notice it, we must (instead of torturing ourselves and wasting our time without any benefit) humble ourselves at once and turn to God with hope, calling to Him from the depths of our heart:

> O Lord my God! I have done this because of my sinful passions. So if Your grace does not help me and I am left to myself, nothing can be expected of me but such sins or even worse. I grieve over what I have done, especially because my life has no righteousness in response to Your care of me. I continue to fall and to fall. Forgive me and give me the strength not to offend You again—and in no way to stray from Your will. For I eagerly wish to work for You, to please You, and to be obedient to You in all things.

We must do this not just once, but, if necessary, a hundred times a day, even every minute—and the last time with the same perfect trust and boldness toward God as the first. In so doing, we will give due honor to the infinite goodness of God, whom we must always see as full of infinite lovingkindness toward us. Then we will never stop making progress in our life and will keep moving forward without waste of time and labor.

Another way of protecting our inner peace when we have given in to these trespasses is the following:

First, combine the inner action of realizing our worthlessness and our humility before God with a warm remembrance of the great mercies God has shown us personally. Thus we rouse in ourselves a desire to thank and glorify Him.

Then, actually thank and glorify Him warmly from the depths of our soul. Since thanking and glorifying God is the highest manifestation of our living union with Him, if we take our downfall properly, its fruit will be (with God's help) our rising higher toward Him.

This should always be kept in view, especially if we are too painfully troubled and tormented by our small transgressions to enable us to see how great our blindness in this matter truly is—and how much we harm ourselves by our bad judgment. It puts into our hands the key with which our soul can open the great treasure house of the spirit and can, in a short time, be enriched by the grace of our Lord Jesus Christ: to whom be glory, honor, and worship, together with His Father who has no beginning, and the Holy Spirit, now and ever and unto ages of ages. Amen.

STUDY QUESTIONS

WHEN PEACE IS INTERRUPTED
1. *What has been your experience with the interruption of*

inner peace? How have you dealt with this?

2. *How can we maintain our courage in the face of the loss of inner peace?*

THE WILES OF THE ENEMY AND INNER PEACE

1. *Consider the means the devil uses to rob us of our inner peace. Have you ever found yourself going along this path? What happened? How did you escape?*

WHEN WE LACK SPIRITUAL FEELINGS

1. *What experiences of spiritual coolness and lack of spiritual joy have you had?*

2. *Given the recommendations in this section, what additional light do you have on your previous experience with these problems?*

EVERY TEMPTATION IS SENT FOR OUR GOOD

1. *What do you do about those thoughts that come to all of us suggesting we are something important?*

2. *Discuss the benefits listed which come through the withdrawal of spiritual comforts, such as feeling closeness to God.*

REMEDY FOR SMALL SINS AND WEAKNESSES

1. *What experience have you had with being discouraged over your besetting sins? How have you handled that discouragement? Given the content of this section, what changes do you think are proper in your means of handling them?*

2. *What is the main ingredient for overcoming excessive distress over common day-to-day sins?*

IF DISTRESSED, CALL OUT!

1. *What are the major weapons given in this section for protecting our inner peace?*

CHAPTER 10

Spiritual Warfare at the Hour of Death

PREPARING FOR THE FINAL BATTLE

Although our whole life on earth is an unceasing warfare, and we have to fight to the very end, the principal and most decisive battle awaits us in the hour of death. In fact, some say that anyone who falls at that moment cannot rise again.

Is that surprising? Don't let it be. The enemy dared even to approach our Lord, who was without sin, at the end of His days on earth, as the Lord Himself said: "The ruler of this world is coming, and he has nothing in Me" (John 14:30). If he dared to so approach the Lord, what can prevent him from attacking us, sinful as we are, at the end of our life?

Saint Basil the Great, in his commentary on the words of the psalm, "Lest they tear me like a lion, rending me in pieces, while there is none to deliver" (Psalm 7:2), says that the most tireless fighters, who have struggled unceasingly with the demons throughout their lives, have avoided their nets and withstood their attacks, are, at the end of their life, subjected to an examination by the prince of this age to see whether anything sinful remains in them. And those who show wounds, or the blots and imprints of sin, are retained in his power, while those who show nothing of this freely pass him by and attain rest with Christ.

Having read such words from such a great Father of the Church, it is imperative that we keep them in view, and prepare ourselves to meet that hour and to pass through it successfully. Indeed, the whole of our life should be a preparation for this. We will be well prepared for this hour if we fight with courage against the enemies of our salvation throughout the whole course of our life on earth. Then, having acquired during our life the skills necessary to overcome our enemies, we will easily be able to acquire the crown of victory in the hour of death.

Furthermore, let us think often of death—with full attention, bringing to mind everything which must happen at that time. If we do this, that hour will not catch us unaware and will not frighten us too much. And our soul, not weakened by fear, will stand more firm and strong to take on the struggle and overcome the enemy.

People of this world run from the thought and memory of death—so as not to interrupt the pleasures and enjoyments of their senses, which are not compatible at all with the memory of death. This makes their attachment to the pleasures of the world grow and strengthen continually, since they encounter nothing opposed to it. But when the time comes to part with life and all the pleasures and things they love, they are thrown into extreme turmoil, terror, and torment.

In order to make this remembrance of death bear its maximum fruit, we must mentally put ourselves in the place of a dying person. Then, in the pain and predicament of mortal agony, we must vividly imagine the enemy temptations which can attack us—at the same time reproducing the thoughts and feelings which have the strength to drive them away.

Soon, we will describe the assaults the enemy may make at that moment and give ways of resisting them, so that, while still alive, we can get used to rehearsing them in our mind, in order to be able to put them into practice when our hour of death comes. For this battle comes only once. And since it is inevitable, we must learn how to meet it and engage in it skillfully, lest we make an irreversible error at the end and suffer losses which cannot be restored.

The four primary and most dangerous temptations to which our enemies, the devil and his demons, usually subject us in the hour of death are:

• wavering or hesitation of faith;
• despair;
• arrogance, pride, and vanity;
• various images simulated by the demons to appear before the dying.

THE FIRST TEMPTATION
IN THE HOUR OF DEATH: AGAINST FAITH

As to the first, when the wicked enemy begins to plant thoughts of unbelief in us—or, appearing in a visible form, speaks to us against faith—we must not enter into an argument with him. Rather, we must affirm within ourselves faith in what he attacks, telling him with holy indignation: "Out of my sight, Satan, father of lies. I refuse to listen to you. With my whole heart and soul I believe and have always believed in what my mother, the Holy Church, believes. And this is enough for me."

We must not allow any thoughts of unbelief, but must stand firm, as the Scriptures say, "If the spirit of the ruler rises against you, do not leave your post; for conciliation pacifies great offenses" (Ecclesiastes 10:4). Further, be vividly aware—and maintain this awareness—that this is nothing but the deceit of the devil, who tries to confuse us in our last hour.

If we cannot stand firm in our spirit, let us keep our desire and feeling alert, not letting them bend toward the suggestion—even if it is served up under the cover of texts from the Scriptures, introduced by the betrayer of souls. For whatever text of the Scriptures he reminds us of, he does so with the aim of leading us to destruction by a distorted interpretation and perversion of the true words of God.

Suppose this evil snake asks us: "What does the Church teach?" We must not answer—and, in fact, should pay no attention to his words, ignoring him altogether. Since we are aware that he is nothing but lies and deceits, and that he has begun to talk to us only to confuse us with words, our best tactic is to plunge deeply into the contemplation of the faith within our believing heart.

If, however, we find ourselves firm in faith and strong in thought—and wish to baffle the enemy—we can answer that the Holy Church believes in the truth alone. Then, if he asks, "What is this truth?" we have an answer: the truth is that in which he himself believes, namely that by the cross our Lord Jesus Christ has struck him on the head and has abolished his power.

Then, with the eye of our spirit, let us cling to the contemplation of our Lord, crucified for us, praying: "O my God, Creator and Redeemer! Come quickly to my aid and do not let me be shaken—however little it may be—in the truth of Your holy faith. Since through Your lovingkindness I was born into this truth, let me remain in it and end my mortal life to the glory of Your name."

THE SECOND TEMPTATION
IN THE HOUR OF DEATH: THROUGH DESPAIR

The second temptation the enemy uses in trying to strike us down in the hour of death is fear at the memory of the multitude of our sins. This fear cannot be avoided—for we are sinners—but it is mitigated by our belief in the redemption of our sins by the death on the cross of Christ our Savior.

The enemy obscures this faith and fans the fear of our sins—in an attempt to crush all hope of salvation and strike us down with hopelessness and despair. Let us therefore prepare ourselves ahead of time to repel this attack, resolving even now to grasp firmly in our hand our victorious banner—the cross of Christ our Savior—when we approach the gates of death.

In other words, keep firmly in your heart faith in the redeeming power of our Lord's death on the cross. If we do actually experience attacks of hopelessness when we enter the gates of death, we must be ready quickly to remember that they are brought on by our enemy and are not the natural result of recalling our sins. The natural result of such recollection is humility, contrition, and heartfelt grief at having offended our righteous and merciful God. So, although this recollection does bring fear, this fear does not destroy our hope in God's mercy.

Actually, when we are joined to this hope, it produces in us a daring and bold trust in salvation, and removes all fear of being cast out. If we know and remember this, we will always recognize as coming from the devil any recollection of our sins which has the power to oppress us and drive us to despair, blotting out all hope of salvation and striking us down through fear of being cast out. Once we are aware of this we will not find it difficult to have hope upon hope—which will drive away all despair.

Hope upon hope immerses us in contemplation of divine mercy. Into the infinite depths of His mercy we must throw the multitude of our sins, with firm conviction that God desires and seeks, not our destruction, but our salvation. There is only one sure foundation on which this conviction can become stronger at any time (and particularly at the time of death): the unlimited power of the death of our Lord and Savior on the cross. Since, therefore, we must always seek the protection of this cross, how much more is it the thing to do in this hour of our death!

Here is a suitable prayer to pray when we are entering the gates of death:

> O Lord! There are so many reasons for me to fear that in Your justice You will condemn me and cast me out for my sins. But there is something still greater: my bold hope in Your forgiveness according to Your infinite mercy in Christ Jesus, our Savior and Redeemer. Therefore I beg You to spare me, Your poor creature, in Your infinite goodness. For

though condemned by my sins, I am washed by the priceless blood of Your Son and our God, to glorify You forever. I give the whole of myself into Your hands. Deal with me in Your mercy. You alone are the Lord of my life.

THE THIRD TEMPTATION IN THE HOUR OF DEATH: THROUGH ARROGANCE AND PRIDE

The third temptation in the hour of death comes through arrogance and pride—self-appreciation—which cause us to rely on ourselves and our own works. Consequently, we must never, especially in the hour of death, let our attention dwell on ourselves and what is ours— giving way to satisfaction with ourselves and our works, even if our progress in virtues happens to be greater than that of all the saints (if that were even possible!).

The solution? Letting all our satisfaction be in God, and placing our hope completely on His mercy and the sufferings of our Lord and Savior. If we wish to be saved, we will belittle ourselves in our own eyes to our last breath. If some good deed we have done comes to mind, let us consider it the work of God in and through us instead of our own work—attributing it entirely to Him.

Here is what we must do: Take refuge in the protection of divine mercy. But we must not allow ourselves to expect it as a reward for the many and difficult struggles we have endured or for the victories we have achieved. We must always stand in the saving fear and sincere conviction that all our efforts, all our struggles and endeavors, would have remained futile and fruitless if God had not taken them under the wing of His kindness, helping and working in them. Thus, it is in His merciful goodness, kindness, and generosity that we trust.

Following this advice, we may be certain that in the hour of death the attack of our enemies will fail and a free road will open before us—a path by which we will pass with joy from the earthly valley to the heavenly Jerusalem, the home we have longed for.

THE FOURTH TEMPTATION IN THE HOUR OF DEATH: THROUGH PHANTOMS OF DEMONS

Our enemy, the devil, is both evil and clever—and he is persistent. If, in his untiring desire to tempt us, he attempts to seduce us in the hour of death by presenting phantoms or visions—or transformation of demons into the appearance of an angel of light—we must stand firm in the consciousness of our poverty and utter insignificance.

We may say to him, from a courageous and fearless heart: "Return to your darkness, accursed one. I know what I see is false, for I am unworthy of visions and revelations. I need just one thing—the infinite compassion of my Lord Jesus Christ and the prayers and intercessions of our Lady, the Mother of God, the Virgin Mary, and of all the saints."

Even if some very clear signs make you think you are seeing a true vision sent by God, don't be quick to believe them. Instead, quickly immerse yourself in the realization of your own insignificance and unworthiness. We must not be afraid we are going to offend God in such situations—humble feelings on our part do not displease Him. God knows how to prevent us from closing our eyes to such visions if we need them. And He will forgive our reluctance to believe they come from Him. He who sends grace to the humble does not take it away for actions inspired by humility.

Visions of this sort are the most usual of the weapons used by our enemy to attack us in our last mortal hour. But he also uses for the same purpose any other passion to which the dying person was susceptible during his life—especially any to which he is most addicted. He attempts to arouse such passions in order to make that person leave this life in a state of passion.

Consequently, we must be armed against our strongest passions before this great battle is upon us—and fighting against them with courage, overcome and cleanse ourselves from them, to make victory easy at our last hour, which may come at any moment. In this connection, the Lord says to us all, "Fight against them until they are consumed" (1 Samuel 15:18).

STUDY QUESTIONS

PREPARING FOR THE FINAL BATTLE
1. *What have you done to prepare yourself for the hour of your death?*
2. *Which of the warnings in this section are most striking to you?*

THE FIRST TEMPTATION
IN THE HOUR OF DEATH: AGAINST FAITH
1. *Have you ever been with anyone at the time of his or her*

death? Did you observe that he or she was being attacked by any of the four temptations listed? If so, which?

2. *What do you feel you need in order to be able to defend yourself from an attack against faith in the hour of death? How can you prepare yourself?*

THE SECOND TEMPTATION IN THE HOUR OF DEATH: THROUGH DESPAIR

1. *What has been your own experience in thinking about the multitude of your sins?*
2. *What specific help do you gain from this section?*
3. *How are you preparing to face this temptation in the hour of your death?*

THE THIRD TEMPTATION IN THE HOUR OF DEATH: THROUGH ARROGANCE AND PRIDE

1. *What has been your experience in trying to rid yourself of pride?*
2. *On what do we trust for the mercy of God?*
3. *What should you be doing to prepare to defeat this temptation in the hour of your death?*

THE FOURTH TEMPTATION IN THE HOUR OF DEATH: THROUGH PHANTOMS OF DEMONS

1. *What experiences have you had of visions? What have you heard from people you know who have experienced them? What is your initial reaction to the advice given here for those on the point of death?*
2. *How should you prepare yourself to fight this temptation in the hour of your death?*

ENDNOTES

1   Throughout this book we refer to our **enemies**. We mean these in particular: the world, the flesh, and the devil. Also included in this term, however, are all the demons of hell, the minions of the devil, those angels who fell with him and desire our downfall as well.

2   Spirit: This word in the Greek text is *nous*, a word usually translated "mind." We think of "mind" as our rational, thinking faculty; but what is meant in this context is something else indeed. *Nous* is a term the spiritual Fathers use frequently to refer to the highest faculty of the soul, through which man can know God. Unlike the reason, which reaches conclusions through deduction, the spirit apprehends divine truth by means of immediate experience or intuition.

Vladimir Lossky describes the spirit as "the seat of the person . . . which contains in itself the whole of man's nature—spirit, soul and body" (*The Mystical Theology of the Eastern Church,* Crestwood, NY: Saint Vladimir's Seminary Press, 1976, p. 201).

3   Passions: Much has been said and written about the passions, from many different points of view. *The Oxford English Dictionary* defines *passion* as "any kind of feeling in which the mind is powerfully affected or moved."

In the "Glossary" of Volume I of the *Philokalia*, our primary source of the writings of the spiritual Fathers of the Church, we find this definition of passion: "In Greek, the

139

word signifies literally that which happens to a person or thing, an experience undergone passively; hence an appetite or impulse such as anger, desire or jealousy, that violently dominates the soul. Many Greek Fathers regard the passions as something intrinsically evil, a 'disease' of the soul: thus St John Klimakos affirms that God is not the creator of the passions and that they are 'unnatural', alien to man's true self ... Other Greek Fathers, however, look on the passions as impulses originally placed in man by God, and so fundamentally good, although at present distorted by sin ... On this second view, then, the passions are to be educated, not eradicated; to be transfigured, not suppressed; to be used positively, not negatively" (*Philokalia*, Vol. I, London: Faber and Faber, 1981, pp. 363-364).

The definition of **dispassion** in the same glossary sheds further light on the subject: "Among the writers of the texts here translated, some regard passion as evil and the consequence of sin, and for them dispassion signifies passionlessness, the uprooting of the passions; others, such as St Isaiah the Solitary, regard the passions as fundamentally good, and for them dispassion signifies a state in which the passions are exercised in accordance with their original purity and so without committing sin in act or thought. Dispassion is a state of reintegration and spiritual freedom; when translating the term into Latin, [John] Cassian rendered it 'purity of heart'. Such a state may imply impartiality and detachment, but not indifference, for if a dispassionate man does not suffer on his own account, he suffers for his fellow creatures. It consists, not in ceasing to feel the attacks of the demons, but in no longer yielding to them. It is positive, not negative: Evagrios links it closely with the quality of love (*agapi*) and Diadochos speaks of the 'fire of dispassion' . . . Dispassion is among the gifts of God" (*Philokalia*, Vol. I, p. 359).

Consequently, we must use great care in speaking of "the passions." We will not consider them as unequivocally evil, but will be very concerned about their misuse. When we speak of "sinful [or ungodly, unwholesome, or misdirected] passions" we will mean: all sorts of illicit desires and passions including hate, improper anger, the lure of illicit sex and the fantasies which accompany it, worry, envy, covetousness, jealousy, self-indulgence—and many other inappropriate and wrong ardent desires and feelings.

Sometimes, however, particularly in later chapters, we will use only the word "passions" when we mean to refer to these "sinful, unwholesome, or misdirected passions."

4 We are writing here of the necessity not to rely on ourselves in spiritual warfare. Ultimately, this applies to every aspect of life—for no part of life is unaffected by the spiritual warfare. And we must always rely on God for everything. We are not saying here, however, that you are to become paralyzed, frozen into inaction, because you cannot rely on yourself. Some things are self-evident: You must rise in the morning, clothe and feed your children, go to work, do your job, etc. In all this, however, learn that it is God upon whom we are to rely in everything we do.

One more thing must be said in this context: We are all of infinite worth in the eyes of God. He values each of us. Thus, we do not consider ourselves worthless. At the same time, there is a self-esteem which is full of pride and arrogance, a self-reliance which is conceited and haughty. These are to be put down within us. Further, no one is ever made worthy or "more worthy"—that is, of greater value—by achievements. It is right for us to do good with our abilities and gifts, but doing so should not raise our self-esteem. In addition, there is a certain sort of pride sometimes taught by modern psychology which also takes our eyes off God and makes us think we are "okay" just as we are. God accepts us as we are, that He might change and remake us according to His will.

5   The **Mysteries** are what are often called the Sacraments—especially Baptism, Chrismation, the Eucharist, Repentance/Confession, Marriage, Ordination, and Holy Unction. Though these comprise what are known as the Seven Holy Mysteries, we must remember that all of life is sacramental and the mysteries of God are innumerable.

6   **Contrition** is not a widely used word today, but it is an extremely important one, not easily replaced. The word comes from the Latin *contritio*, which means "a breaking of something hardened." How appropriate! Ezekiel writes the words of the Lord, "I do not desire the death of the wicked, but that the wicked turn from his way and live" (Ezekiel 33:11). And our Lord said, "Unless you repent you will all likewise perish" (Luke 13:5). He also reports that the prodigal son said to his father, "Father, I have sinned against heaven and in your sight, and am no longer worthy to be called your son" (Luke 15:21). This is that

depth of interior repentance which has been called "contrition." It involves sorrow deep within the soul and a hatred of the sin committed, as well as a steadfast intent not to sin in the future. Sorrow and remorse in the sense of mental agreement are not enough, nor is an intent to improve. Contrition involves learning pain and bitterness of soul, as well as hatred and even horror toward the sin committed.

7   This admonition is not meant to forbid any of us from taking reasonable care and pains about things required by our condition and position in life—since such attention is in conformity with God's will and does not interfere with inner peace, devotion to God, or our progress in the spirit. We simply have to take care of certain things, make arrangements for future travel, future events, and so forth. God knows this. We may and must take care; but we must trust God for the result of our labors.

INDEX

A

activities, spiritual. *See* practices, devout
afflictions
    dealing with   35–37
    endurance of   57–59, 93–94
    prayer in time of   79
    sent as test   17–18, 36–37
    sent for instruction   23, 26, 58
    sent for purification   36
agitation of heart, avoiding   35–37
angels of light, demons pose as   24, 59, 136
anxiety   31, 38, 94, 103, 107
arrogance. *See* pride
ascetic practices. *See* practices, devout
attachment. *See* passions: attachment of

B

Basil the Great   129
bitterness   77, 108, 117, 120, 124
blindness, spiritual   41, 45–46, 126
body
    attention to   72–76
    discipline of   14, 60–62
    obedient to spirit   82
    of Christ   68
    proper state of   44
burnt offering. *See* sacrifice of oneself to God

C

Christ
    following   15, 79, 112
    mercy of   134, 136
    our redemption by   133
    suffering with   96, 112
    sufferings of   17, 79, 106–107, 112
    victory over devil   132

R
relationship
  four types of   81
  to God   82
  to material things   83
  to neighbors   83
  to oneself   82
remorse for sins   18
renunciation   27, 71, 85, 104
repentance   31, 36, 39–42, 71, 84–88, 124–125
  danger of delaying   46–50
resolution   48, 86, 121
rest in God   108
reward   104
righteous deeds. *See* practices, devout

S
sacrament of confession   31
sacraments   142
sacrifice of oneself to God   69, 79, 108–109
saints   55, 59–62, 109, 111, 135–136
salvation   17, 28, 47–50, 59, 67, 84–88, 90, 96, 98, 104, 130
  hope of   133–134
  of others   102–104
Scriptures
  devil's use of   132
  reading   106–107
self-admiration   23
self-appreciation   113, 135
self-condemnation   40, 86
self-control   35
self-deception   53–55
self-delusion   44
self-denial   15, 18, 72, 76, 80, 98–99
self-esteem   22–26, 29, 31, 38, 142
self-examination   84–88
self-glorification   118
self-gratification   63
self-importance   63
self-indulgence   38, 61–62, 78, 85–88

W

warmth of heart, spiritual
   definition of   71–76
   preserving   72–76
   restoring   77–81
   source of   71–76
weakness, human   18–19, 24–26, 30–31, 37, 48–50, 81, 97,
      117, 120, 123–125, 127
weapons for spiritual warfare   20–21, 47
will of God, submission to   18–19, 36–37, 58–59, 67–69, 76–
      81, 93–94, 96, 103–104, 104–107, 109, 111–112
will, one's own
   obedient to spirit   82
   renouncing   18, 98–99
   weakness of   48–50
worries   72, 104
worry   94, 106

Z

zeal   19, 55, 60, 72–76, 80, 86, 97, 103–104, 114, 117
   false   97–98, 102